Standardized Test Tutor

SCHOLASTIC

GRADE **5**

READING

Practice Tests With Question-by-Question Strategies and Tips That Help Students Build Test-Taking Skills and Boost Their Scores

Michael Priestley

Editor: Maria L. Chang
Cover design by Brian LaRossa
Interior design by Creative Pages, Inc.
Illustrations by Wilkinson Studios, Inc.
Photos: page 47: © Bruce Coleman Inc./Alamy; page 49: © Danita Delimont/Alamy

ISBN-13: 978-0-545-09603-4
ISBN-10: 0-545-09603-0
Copyright © 2009 by Michael Priestley
All rights reserved.
Printed in the U.S.A.

1   2   3   4   5   6   7   8   9   10   40   15   14   13   12   11   10   09

Contents

Welcome to *Test Tutor*!

Students in schools today take a lot of tests, especially in reading and math. Some students naturally perform well on tests, and some do not. But just about everyone can get better at taking tests by learning more about what's on the test and how to answer the questions. How many students do you know who could benefit from working with a tutor? How many would love to have someone sit beside them and help them work their way through the tests they have to take?

That's where *Test Tutor* comes in. The main purpose of *Test Tutor* is to help students learn what they need to know in order to do better on tests. Along the way, *Test Tutor* will help students feel more confident as they come to understand the content and learn some of the secrets of success for multiple-choice tests.

The Test Tutor series includes books for reading and books for math in a range of grades. Each Test Tutor book in reading has three full-length practice tests designed specifically to resemble the state tests that students take each year. The reading skills measured on these practice tests have been selected from an analysis of the skills tested in ten major states, and the questions have been written to match the multiple-choice format used in most states.

The most important feature of this book is the friendly Test Tutor. He will help students work through the tests and achieve the kind of success they are looking for. This program is designed so students may work through the tests independently by reading the Test Tutor's helpful hints. Or you may work with the student as a tutor yourself, helping him or her understand each question and test-taking strategy along the way. You can do this most effectively by following the Test Tutor's guidelines included in the pages of this book.

Three Different Tests

There are three practice tests in this book: Test 1, Test 2, and Test 3. Each test has 40 multiple-choice items with four answer choices (A, B, C, D). All three tests measure the same skills, but they provide different levels of tutoring help.

Test 1 provides step-by-step guidance to help students find the answer to each question, as in the sample on the next page. The tips in Test 1 are detailed and thorough. Some of the tips are designed to help students read through and understand the passage, and others are written specifically for each reading question to help students figure out the answers.

Sample 1

Directions: Read this passage about hatching eggs. Then answer questions 6–11.

Hatching Eggs Without a Hen

In nature, most birds' eggs hatch after the mother bird sits on them for several weeks. Farmers and scientists have learned how to hatch eggs without a mother's help. Hatching an egg at home is an interesting science experiment.

The first step is to buy or borrow an incubator. This is a machine that keeps eggs warm while the tiny creatures inside develop. Since eggs must be turned several times a day in order to hatch, many incubators contain turning mechanisms. If your machine lacks one of these devices, you will need to turn your eggs by hand. Make sure the incubator is clean if it is not brand-new. Remove all feathers, shells, or other material with a vacuum cleaner. Then wash with detergent and rinse with a disinfectant. Make sure the incubator is dry before putting in the eggs.

Take a quick look at the questions before you begin reading. See if there are any questions you can answer without reading the passage. But don't answer them yet.

6. Which two words from this passage are synonyms?

Ⓐ *incubate* and *borrow*

Ⓑ *mechanism* and *device*

Ⓒ *coating* and *contents*

Ⓓ *germ* and *disease*

Remember that synonyms are words that have the same meaning.

Test 2 provides a test-taking tip for each item, as in the sample on the next page, but the tips are less detailed than in Test 1. They help guide the student toward the answers without giving away too much. Students must take a little more initiative.

Sample 2

Directions: Read this passage about some unusual living things. Then answer questions 1–5.

Fungi

Every living thing on Earth is either a plant or an animal, right? Wrong! Many organisms in our world are neither. Some of these mysterious inhabitants float invisibly through the air, and some lie hidden in the ground. They do not need sunlight to survive, and if the weather becomes too cold, they can become dormant until conditions improve.

What are these creatures? They are called fungi, and you see them almost every day. Many kinds of fungi seem disgusting, such as the yucky green and moldy black stuff that sprouts on food left too long in the refrigerator. But other kinds are not so bad. For example, the yeast that bakers use to make bread rise is a type of fungus. Mushrooms are also fungi.

> Take a quick look at the questions before you begin reading.

3. The author most likely wrote this passage to—
   (A) help readers recognize fungi in the wild.
   (B) tell an entertaining story about people and fungi.
   (C) give information about fungi.
   (D) compare mushrooms to other kinds of fungi.

> Think about the purpose of the passage as a whole.

Test 3 does not provide test-taking tips. It assesses the progress students have made. After working through Tests 1 and 2 with the help of the Test Tutor, students should be more than ready to score well on Test 3 without too much assistance. Success on this test will help students feel confident and prepared for taking real tests.

Other Helpful Features

In addition to the tests, this book provides some other helpful features. First, on page 73, you will find an **answer sheet**. When students take the tests, they may mark their answers by filling in bubbles on the test pages. Or they may mark their answers on a copy of the answer sheet instead, as they will be required to do in most standardized tests. You may want to have students mark their answers on the test pages for Test 1 and then use an answer sheet for Tests 2 and 3 to help them get used to filling in bubbles.

Second, beginning on page 74, you will find a detailed **answer key** for each test. The answer key lists the correct (and incorrect) responses and explains the answer. It also identifies the skill tested by the question, as in the sample below.

Answer Key for Sample 1

Correct response: **B**
(*Identify synonyms*)
　　Mechanism and *device* have almost the same meaning, so they are synonyms.

Incorrect choices:

A *Incubate* and *borrow* have very different meanings; they are not synonyms.

C The *coating* on the outside of an egg and the *contents* (on the inside) are not the same.

D *Germ* and *disease* are related to each other but do not mean the same thing.

As the sample indicates, this question measures the student's ability to identify synonyms. This information can help you determine which skills the student has mastered and which ones still cause difficulty.

Finally, the answer key explains why each incorrect answer choice, or "distractor," is incorrect. This explanation can help reveal what error the student might have made. For example, a question about an effect might have a distractor that describes a cause instead. Knowing this could help the student improve his or her understanding of the text.

At the back of this book, you will find two scoring charts. The **Student Scoring Chart** can be used to help keep track of each student's scores on all three tests and on each passage (literary or informational). The **Classroom Scoring Chart** can be used to record the scores for all students on all three tests, illustrating the progress they have made from Test 1 to Test 3. Ideally, students should score higher on each test as they go through them. However, keep in mind that students get a lot of tutoring help on Test 1, some help on Test 2, and no help on Test 3. So if a student's scores on all three tests are all fairly similar, that could still be a positive sign that the student is better able to read passages and answer comprehension questions independently and will achieve even greater success on future tests.

Read each passage and the questions that follow. Look at the Test Tutor's tips for understanding the passages and answering the questions. Then choose the best answer to each question.

Test Tutor says:

Directions: Read this passage about a boy who makes birthday cards. Then answer questions 1–5.

The Card Maker

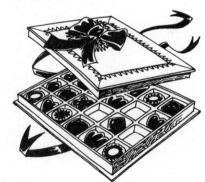

Every year Edwin asked his grandmother what she wanted for her birthday. Every year she told him her favorite present was a homemade birthday card. He had made one decorated with macaroni and one with blinking lights. Last year he had made one four feet tall with an envelope to match. This year he had planned to make her a card the size of his thumb with a greeting she would need a microscope to read! However, when he tried to cut it out of colored paper, he kept messing up.

Edwin also knew that his grandma loved candy, so he went to the drugstore and bought a big box of assorted chocolates. Unfortunately, he bought it a week before her birthday. It sat on his dresser, day after day, tempting him. Edwin had inherited his grandmother's sweet tooth.

The night before her birthday, Edwin decided he should make sure the chocolates were nice and fresh. Sometimes things sat on the drugstore shelves too long. He untied the stiff gold ribbon, slit the plastic wrap, and lifted the lid.

Inside, dozens of chocolates beamed up at him. Each looked slightly different, but all looked delicious. A diagram identified each variety. The first one in the top row was "coconut."

Grandma hated coconut! To save her from accidentally eating it, Edwin grabbed the piece of candy and stuffed it into his mouth. But it wasn't coconut, it was almond—one of Grandma's favorites! Edwin found the actual coconut candy and ate it, too.

Two empty spaces stared up at him like missing teeth in a 6-year-old's smile. Grandma's present no longer looked shiny and

Before you read the passage, take a quick look at the questions so you know what to look for.

Think about Edwin's plan for his grandmother's birthday and what he will probably do.

What kind of person is Edwin?

Standardized Test Tutor: Reading (Grade 5) © 2009 by Michael Priestley, Scholastic Teaching Resources

appetizing. It looked like something that had been sitting around on the coffee table. Edwin felt a hollow space in his stomach. To fill it, he grabbed another chocolate. It had a cherry inside. Then he stopped. He felt terrible. It was too late to go back to the drugstore. What could he do?

Looking around, he saw the art supplies he had planned to use on the card. Then he realized something. Each empty space in the chocolate box was just about the size of his thumb! He carried the supplies to the kitchen table and got started.

What happens in the end?

Questions 1–5: Choose the best answer to each question.

1. What will Edwin most likely do next?

(A) He will make Grandma a card and keep the chocolates for himself.

(B) He will write an apology to Grandma for eating her candy.

(C) He will bake a cake and decorate it with some of the chocolates.

(D) He will make three tiny cards and put them in the empty spaces.

Look at the ending of the story and think about what Edwin had originally planned to do.

2. What can you tell about Edwin from this story?

(A) He is greedy but kindhearted.

(B) He is creative but lazy.

(C) He is honest but dull.

(D) He is sad but determined.

Go back to the fifth and sixth paragraphs to see how Edwin acts.

3. The passage says, "Two empty spaces stared up at him like missing teeth in a 6-year-old's smile." This sentence is an example of—

(A) hyperbole.

(B) a metaphor.

(C) personification.

(D) a simile.

Notice that this sentence compares two things that are different and uses the word *like* to compare them.

4. Why did Edwin eat the cherry chocolate?

　Ⓐ　Cherry is his favorite flavor.

　Ⓑ　He was upset.

　Ⓒ　Grandma hates that kind of chocolate.

　Ⓓ　He wanted to see if it was fresh.

5. The author's main purpose in this passage is to—

　Ⓐ　explain how to make a homemade birthday card.

　Ⓑ　remind people to give their grandparents birthday presents.

　Ⓒ　teach an important lesson about showing respect for older people.

　Ⓓ　tell an entertaining story about a boy and some candy.

Go back to the passage to see how Edwin felt right before he ate the chocolate.

Think about why the author wrote this passage.

Standardized Test Tutor: Reading (Grade 5) © 2009 by Michael Priestley, Scholastic Teaching Resources

Directions: Read this passage about hatching eggs. Then answer questions 6–11.

Hatching Eggs Without a Hen

In nature, most birds' eggs hatch after the mother bird sits on them for several weeks. Farmers and scientists have learned how to hatch eggs without a mother's help. Hatching an egg at home is an interesting science experiment.

The first step is to buy or borrow an incubator. This is a machine that keeps eggs warm while the tiny creatures inside develop. Since eggs must be turned several times a day in order to hatch, many incubators contain turning mechanisms. If your machine lacks one of these devices, you will need to turn your eggs by hand. Make sure the incubator is clean if it is not brand-new. Remove all feathers, shells, or other material with a vacuum cleaner. Then wash with detergent and rinse with a disinfectant. Make sure the incubator is dry before putting in the eggs.

Next, you need to buy or select your eggs. You can go to a poultry farm, or you can buy eggs over the Internet as easily as buying a pair of sneakers!

Conditions must be correct in order for eggs to incubate successfully. The temperature and the humidity must be correct, and there must be enough ventilation (fresh air). Use the table on the next page to determine the correct conditions for your eggs.

Tips on Egg Selection:

- Eggs should come from mature, healthy hens.
- Avoid eggs that are especially large or small.
- Do not select eggs with cracked shells.
- Pick eggs with a smooth, oval shape. Avoid oddly shaped eggs.
- Avoid very dirty eggs. If eggs are a little dirty, that's okay. An egg has a protective coating designed to keep germs from hurting its contents. DO NOT WASH THE EGG! Washing will remove this coating and allow disease to pass through the shell.

Take a quick look at the questions before you begin reading. See if there are any questions you can answer without reading the passage. But don't answer them yet.

What is this passage mainly about?

Type of egg	Incubation period (days)	Temperature (Fahrenheit)	Humidity (%)	Last day for turning eggs
chicken	21	100	85–87	18th day
turkey	28	99	84–86	25th day
duck	28	100	85–86	25th day
goose	28–34	99	86–88	25th day

> How can this table help you? What kinds of information does this table give?

At the end of the incubation period, the real excitement begins. The chick uses its sharp beak to break its way out of the shell. This can be a real battle lasting many hours! The chick will be wet and sticky when it emerges, but it will use its beak to clean and fluff up its feathers. Then it will be ready for some water to drink and special poultry food to eat. Keep baby birds safe by giving them water in a shallow dish.

Questions 6–11: Choose the best answer to each question.

6. Which two words from this passage are synonyms?

   (A) *incubate* and *borrow*

   (B) *mechanism* and *device*

   (C) *coating* and *contents*

   (D) *germ* and *disease*

> Remember that synonyms are words that have the same meaning.

7. Which action would most likely result in an unhealthy egg?

   (A) cleaning an egg with dish detergent

   (B) turning an egg by hand instead of by machine

   (C) sending an egg through the mail

   (D) not turning an egg just before it hatches

> Use the text and the tips listed in the box to find the answer.

8. Which type of egg takes the longest time to hatch?

   (A) chicken

   (B) turkey

   (C) duck

   (D) goose

> Look at the table to find the answer.

Standardized Test Tutor: Reading (Grade 5) © 2009 by Michael Priestley, Scholastic Teaching Resources

9. What happens just after the chick breaks out of its shell?

(A) It drinks some water.

(B) It eats some food.

(C) It cleans its feathers.

(D) It lays an egg.

Go back to the last paragraph in the passage to see what happens.

10. The passage says that you should rinse the incubator with a *disinfectant*. The word *disinfectant* means—

(A) "a person who cleans things."

(B) "something that kills germs."

(C) "a place where germs grow."

(D) "like or related to an egg."

Look at the parts of the word to figure out what it means.

11. What conclusion can be drawn from this passage?

(A) Problems in the way an egg looks suggest that it will have trouble hatching.

(B) Eggs that are kept warm by a mother bird are much healthier than eggs kept warm in an incubator.

(C) Different types of birds have different methods of escaping from their eggshells.

(D) Baby birds can either clean their feathers with their beaks or go for a swim in a dish or bowl.

Read each answer carefully and check the passage for information.

Directions: Read this poem about a painter. Then answer questions 12–17.

Ronald the Painter

Ronald the Painter is painting our house;
He's been working for seven long days.
My mom wishes he would work like a mouse,
But he's loud like a donkey that brays.

He stands on his ladder and surveys the scene   5
And nothing escapes his sharp gaze.
He comments whenever we go in or out,
And he's been here for seven long days.

"Hey, Joseph!" he shouts when I open the door.
(There is nothing I hate like a fuss.)   10
"Hey, buddy, how goes it?" he yells from on high,
And I cringe as I wait for the bus.

At noontime the postman drives by in his truck,
And my mother steps out for the mail.
"Whadja get, same old junk?" Ronald asks with a grin, 15
And he asks this each day without fail.

When my sister Rebecca goes out to her swing,
Ronald calls, "Hey, Rebecca, knock-knock!"
Rebecca's so little she stares at the door,
But the painter explains it's a joke.   20

On Saturday morning we all creep out the back
Because Ronald works Saturdays, too.
"Hey, guys, check it out!" booms that familiar voice,
So we sigh and go see what is new.

He's stepped off his ladder; he's beaming with pride   25
At the side of our house that is done.
The walls are bright yellow, the trim gleaming white—
Our old house looks as bright as the sun.

But what's wrong with the door? It's all covered with spots:
Evergreen, cherry red, midnight blue . . .   30
"Pick your fave, take your time, I won't charge!"
Ron explains, "A cool door is my present to you!"

> As you read, notice what characteristics make this selection a poem.

> What is happening in this poem?

> Notice how the members of the family feel about Ronald.

> What does Ron do for the family?

Standardized Test Tutor: Reading (Grade 5) © 2009 by Michael Priestley, Scholastic Teaching Resources

"Knock-knock!" says Rebecca, and everyone laughs,
Then we analyze each different hue.
It takes us a while to come up with our choice,   35
But we finally say, "Midnight blue."

"Awesome choice," nods Big Ronald, "you guys have great taste,"
Then he picks up his brush and his pail.
"The weather is changing, there's no time to waste!
I must finish Thursday without fail."   40

On Monday I wave as I wait for the bus,
On Tuesday Mom shows him the mail,
Wednesday Beck tells him a joke that she learned,
But on Thursday there's wind, rain, and hail.

> What change takes place in this stanza?

On Friday the sun is back and so is Ron,   45
But he's quiet and sad—what is wrong?
It turns out that he promised to beat the big storm,
And he feels that his work took too long.

"Your work is just perfect," my mother explains,
"Our last painter was really a slob!"   50
"And we like the blue door," I loudly exclaim.
"And the hail didn't damage the job!"

So Ron finishes, puts his gear in the van,
And blushes at all of our praise.

> What happens at the end?

We cannot believe he won't work here next week;   55
He's been here fourteen wonderful days!

—*Stacey Sparks*

Questions 12–17: Choose the best answer to each question.

12. What is the meaning of the word *hue* in line 34?

> Look for clues in the lines before and after the word.

Ⓐ paint

Ⓑ idea

Ⓒ gift

Ⓓ color

13. Which characteristic does this poem have?

Ⓐ two different settings

Ⓑ many metaphors and similes

Ⓒ lines that rhyme

Ⓓ animal characters that talk

> Check each answer choice by going back to the poem.

14. How do Joseph's feelings change over the course of the poem?

Ⓐ At first he does not trust Ron, but eventually he does.

Ⓑ At first he is annoyed by Ron, but eventually he likes Ron.

Ⓒ At first he admires Ron, but then he feels sorry for Ron.

Ⓓ At first he scarcely notices Ron, but then he pays attention to Ron.

> Read the first three and last four stanzas to see what change takes place.

15. Which adjective best describes Ron?

Ⓐ friendly

Ⓑ shy

Ⓒ lazy

Ⓓ polite

> Read all the answer choices carefully. Consider each choice and cross out the ones you know to be wrong.

16. What happens on Thursday?

Ⓐ Rain and hail keep Ron from working.

Ⓑ Joseph and his family creep out the back.

Ⓒ Rebecca tells Ron a joke.

Ⓓ Members of the family choose blue for the door.

> Look at lines 41 to 44 to see what happens.

17. Why does Ron feel unhappy toward the end of the poem?

Ⓐ He realizes he has been making too much noise.

Ⓑ He thinks the door is the wrong color.

Ⓒ He thinks he should have worked faster.

Ⓓ He worries that he is going to miss the family.

> Review the last three stanzas to find the answer.

Standardized Test Tutor: Reading (Grade 5) © 2009 by Michael Priestley, Scholastic Teaching Resources

Directions: Read this passage about an unusual crime. Then answer questions 18–24.

Police Arrest Unruly Neighbors

MOUNT GILEAD, Ohio—A local dispute between neighbors has finally led to arrests, according to police sources. Yesterday afternoon, Ryan Southpaw and Jerome Levesque, both of Melody Lane, were charged with disturbing the peace. They were taken into custody.

The latest episode in the ongoing battle began June 20. Mr. Southpaw backed a truck onto Mr. Levesque's driveway and dumped dozens of lawn ornaments onto the asphalt. This prevented Mr. Levesque from driving his daughter April to soccer practice.

Mr. Levesque retaliated by opening the windows of his house and blasting heavy metal music at top volume. He then started heaving the ornaments into Mr. Southpaw's yard. Mr. Southpaw aimed his speakers at his neighbor's house. The ammunition was opera. He then stormed out of his garage and hurled the ornaments in the other direction. One painted dwarf formed a large crater in the Levesques' flower bed. A pink flamingo landed in a cherry tree.

Neighbors called the police.

One woman, who refused to give her name, said, "It's a pity. These boys grew up together. They used to be such good friends."

The problem started a year ago.

Mr. Levesque got a bumper sticker that said, "Proud Father of a Middle School Soccer Star." April Levesque is on the local club team. She is also on the regional travel team Mr. Levesque coaches.

Mr. Southpaw then got his own bumper sticker. It said, "Honk if you're tired of bragging parents."

Mr. Levesque complained that this was meant to mock him. He then bought an electric sign for his front yard. It said, "Even Prouder Parent of a Soccer Star!"

Mr. Southpaw called Town Hall. He complained that his neighbor had an illegal sign in his yard. He said that electric signs are only allowed in the central business district. The town ordered Mr. Levesque to remove the electric sign.

Mr. Levesque replaced the sign with a large playhouse. The front door said, "Welcome to the Soccer Star's Playhouse."

Scan the questions before you read so you know what to look for.

What happened to make these neighbors upset?

What does the writer/reporter think of this situation?

Mr. Southpaw checked the local regulations. Playhouses, sheds, and other small buildings must be located in backyards, so Mr. Levesque was forced to relocate the structure.

This spring, Ollie's Garden Center in nearby Ford Creek went out of business. Mr. Levesque bought up their entire stock of concrete bunnies. He painted tears on their faces and planted them on his front lawn. All faced Mr. Southpaw's house.

"We all got the message," says another neighbor. "It was, 'Shame on you.'"

Local officials say Mr. Southpaw began haunting Town Hall. He combed the zoning regulations, searching for an anti-concrete-bunny rule. None existed.

James Kershaw of Jim's Rent-a-Truck was willing to speak on the record. "I knew Ryan was getting bent out of shape over this. He kept saying the police wouldn't do anything. I pointed out that they couldn't. There's nothing illegal about decorating your yard with lawn ornaments. I should have known something was up when Ryan rented a dump truck. Frankly, Ryan's not a dump truck kind of guy.

He said he needed it for some gravel. I should have said no."

Ryan Southpaw drove the rented truck to Garden Giant. According to the manager, Robin Wright, he bought 20 items.

"Some of them were quite lovely," Wright says. "We offered to wrap them, but he said no. He just threw them in the back of the truck."

According to police reports, Southpaw did not try to hide his actions. After dumping the ornaments, he yelled, "You like ornaments? Here are some ornaments! Ornaments, ornaments, ornaments!"

Listeners called in to local radio station WGPP with suggestions on how to stop the conflict. One woman suggested that the two men go to Betty's Pie Palace to discuss matters. "It's just impossible to stay angry over a piece of that heavenly pie," she said.

Psychologist Dr. Leonard Makin offered his services. "I think both men have issues," he said.

A court date has not yet been set.

> What happens at the end?

Standardized Test Tutor: Reading (Grade 5) © 2009 by Michael Priestley, Scholastic Teaching Resources

Questions 18–24: Choose the best answer to each question.

18. The passage says, "Mr. Levesque *retaliated* by opening the windows of his house and blasting heavy metal music at top volume." The word *retaliated* means—

Ⓐ "backed down."

Ⓑ "complained about."

Ⓒ "asked for sympathy."

Ⓓ "fought back."

> Look for clues in the second and third paragraphs to help find the meaning.

19. What is the main idea of this passage?

Ⓐ Two neighbors compete over who can have the best-landscaped lawn.

Ⓑ Differing tastes in music cause an ongoing battle between neighbors.

Ⓒ Former friends become enemies after one reacts negatively to the other's bumper sticker.

Ⓓ Town officials arrest two former friends for disturbing the peace.

> To find the main idea, think about what the whole passage is mostly about.

20. Which sentence states an opinion?

Ⓐ "These boys grew up together."

Ⓑ "We all got the message."

Ⓒ "There's nothing illegal about decorating your yard with lawn ornaments."

Ⓓ "Some of them were quite lovely."

> Remember, an opinion gives a personal view or feeling that cannot be proven true.

21. Why did Mr. Southpaw get upset in the first place?

Ⓐ He thought Mr. Levesque was bragging too much about his daughter.

Ⓑ He did not like listening to heavy metal music.

Ⓒ He could not sleep at night because of Mr. Levesque's electric sign.

Ⓓ He thought his neighbor's lawn ornaments were ugly.

> Look back at the passage to see how the problem started.

22. What is the reporter's point of view toward the events described in this passage?

Ⓐ horrified

Ⓑ sad

Ⓒ amused

Ⓓ furious

> Think about how the reporter describes the events that take place.

23. The passage says, "I knew Ryan was getting bent out of shape over this." What is the meaning of *getting bent out of shape*?

Ⓐ planning something destructive

Ⓑ becoming really upset

Ⓒ being physically damaged

Ⓓ looking for help

> Think about how Ryan Southpaw feels to help figure out the meaning of this phrase.

24. Which detail supports the idea that there was nothing the police could do about the painted bunnies that faced Mr. Southpaw's house?

Ⓐ Ollie's Garden Center went out of business.

Ⓑ Ryan Southpaw began haunting Town Hall.

Ⓒ There were no laws against concrete bunnies.

Ⓓ Ryan Southpaw made no effort to hide his actions.

> Read each answer choice carefully and think about why the police could not act.

Standardized Test Tutor: Reading (Grade 5) © 2009 by Michael Priestley, Scholastic Teaching Resources

Test Tutor says:

Directions: Read this passage about how grass came to be. Then answer questions 25–32.

The Birth of the Green World

Long ago, most of Earth was covered in smooth, gray rock. Here and there, small plants and bushes grew in cracks in the rocks. Birds and animals fed on the berries and leaves from these plants and bushes, and so did a few people.

> What kind of passage begins like this?

Back in those days, Earth was ruled by gods who needed no earthly food to survive. They feasted on air and starshine, and never grew sick or old. They laughed when they saw humans searching desperately for green plants to eat. They did not understand why humans did not eat clouds and shadows, which were so plentiful and delicious.

One afternoon, Mira, the daughter of the great god Hall, was walking in a valley near her home on Mount Gorash. She walked barefoot, enjoying the warmth of stone soaked in sunlight. She was looking up for a sunbeam to snack on when suddenly she felt something sharp prick her foot. She cried out in pain. She had accidentally stepped on a small, thorny plant poking out of a crevice in the rock, and a thorn pierced the sole of her foot.

> What causes a problem in this passage?

Furious, she stumbled back home and showed her father the tiny cut.

"Get rid of all the plants!" she demanded. "This must never happen again!"

Hall called upon the Weavers of Dorn, who lived in a cave at the foot of Mount Gorash and spun fabric for the gods' clothes, bedding, and furniture. "Make a carpet that will cover the entire world," he commanded.

> How did Hall try to solve the problem?

The weavers worked for 30 days and 30 nights, making a carpet as wide as the world and as gray as fog. When they were finished, all of the gods lifted up an edge of the rug and rolled it out until it covered the entire globe.

How happy Mira was! Now she could run and frolic wherever she liked without fear of another terrible thorn! Because she was happy, Hall was happy. Because the leader of the gods was happy, all the rest of the gods were contented.

So imagine how puzzled they were the morning after the rug was unrolled, when they heard a sound of wailing so loud it rose to the peak of Mount Gorash.

"What is that racket?" grumbled Hall to his servant Fen, for although gods could dine on air, they needed sleep.

Fen trudged down the mountain, which was covered by the carpet, to the valley, which was covered likewise. To his surprise, a small group of humans was waiting there. As he approached, a thin, red-haired man with a small, red-haired daughter spoke up.

"Oh, mighty creature!" the man said. This pleased Fen, for he was used to getting little respect among the gods. "Tell us, what is this terrible substance that covers the world? If it remains, everything living will blow away like a puff of smoke—the plants, the rabbits, the bees, and the people. We cannot survive without food!"

Fen did not know what the man was talking about, but he did not want to admit this. He liked being looked up to and treated as all-knowing.

"My lady Mira hurt her foot on a thorn," he explained to the funny little people who looked at him so sadly. "This carpet makes the world soft for her and all gentle creatures. My lord Hall will never put things back the way they used to be."

The small, red-haired girl pointed to something green that poked through the carpet. It was a single blade of grass. "Why not cover the earth with grass?" she asked. "Grass is even softer than this carpet, it is more beautiful because it is green and alive, and it smells sweet after a rain. I'm sure Mira would love it."

Fen carried the little girl's message back to Hall, who liked the idea of covering the earth with something that his daughter would enjoy even more than the carpet. He consulted with Yar, the wisest god, who said that grass likes rain, and that if Fen rolled up the carpet, and Graybeak the Rain God produced more rain, the grass would flourish.

All of this came to pass. The rain watered the grass, the grass fed the animals, the animals fed the people, and people thrived until they covered Earth.

Of course, the thorns grew back as well, so Mira and the other gods eventually decided they were happier on Mount Gorash where the grass never grew. And that is why you never see the gods walking among us anymore.

How do the people feel about what has happened?

Standardized Test Tutor: Reading (Grade 5) © 2009 by Michael Priestley, Scholastic Teaching Resources

Standardized Test Tutor: Reading (Grade 5) © 2009 by Michael Priestley, Scholastic Teaching Resources

Questions 25–32: Choose the best answer to each question.

25. What is the main conflict in this story?

   Ⓐ The animals and the humans are fighting over food.

   Ⓑ Mira wants to leave her home, but her father wants to keep her there.

   Ⓒ The gods want to get rid of plants, but humans need them.

   Ⓓ People and gods are fighting over who should rule Earth.

> Go back to the passage to see what the gods and the humans disagree about.

26. Which character suggests a way to resolve the main conflict?

   Ⓐ Mira

   Ⓑ Hall

   Ⓒ the red-haired girl

   Ⓓ Graybeak the Rain God

> Look back at the story to find the answer.

27. Where was Mira when she hurt her foot?

   Ⓐ on top of a mountain

   Ⓑ in a valley

   Ⓒ in a cave

   Ⓓ at home

> Check the third paragraph to find the answer.

28. In this passage, how are the gods different from humans?

   Ⓐ They do not feel pain.

   Ⓑ They do not eat.

   Ⓒ They do not sleep.

   Ⓓ They do not die.

> Read each answer choice carefully and check it against the passage.

Standardized Test Tutor: Reading (Grade 5) © 2009 by Michael Priestley, Scholastic Teaching Resources

29. Why does Hall decide to cover Earth with grass?

Ⓐ He wants the people to be quiet so he can sleep.

Ⓑ He realizes that the animals cannot live without plants to eat.

Ⓒ He wants to make the world more pleasant for his daughter.

Ⓓ He wants to prove to the rest of the gods that he is wise.

> Look near the end of the story to see why Hall does this.

30. What does the red-haired man mean when he says, "Everything living will blow away like a puff of smoke"?

Ⓐ Everything on Earth will die if the carpet remains.

Ⓑ The carpet is the color of smoke.

Ⓒ Someone will accidentally set the carpet on fire.

Ⓓ The people will forget what the world was like before the carpet.

> Look for clues in the sentences before and after this one.

31. This story is an example of—

Ⓐ a biography.

Ⓑ science fiction.

Ⓒ a myth.

Ⓓ realistic fiction.

> Think about what happens in the story. Which of the choices is the most likely answer?

32. Which sentence expresses a theme of this story?

Ⓐ Every cloud has a silver lining.

Ⓑ There is more than one way to solve a problem.

Ⓒ When things go wrong, it is best to be patient.

Ⓓ Ignoring a problem just makes it worse.

> Remember that the theme is the message, or lesson, the author wants you to learn.

Directions: Read these two passages about bread. Then answer questions 33–40.

Passage 1: Bread

A Long History

Bread has been a staple, or basic food, in Europe, parts of Africa, and the Middle East for thousands of years. Archaeologists have found 5,000-year-old loaves in Egyptian tombs. In ancient Greece, bakers from different regions argued about who baked the tastiest bread.

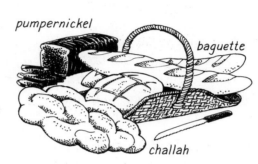

pumpernickel

baguette

challah

In ancient Rome, bakers enjoyed special privileges because their product was so valued. During the Middle Ages, strict laws were passed to control the production and sale of bread, and prices were kept low so that everyone could afford this important food.

In medieval times, most bakers were proud of their craft and very honest, but a few found creative ways to cheat the public. In one English bake house, customers used to bring raw loaves to be baked. In 1327, some dishonest bakers made secret openings in the counters where the loaves were placed. They then pinched off small amounts of dough through these openings and used it to make their own loaves! When they were caught, they were forced to sit in a pillory wearing "necklaces" of dough around their necks!

The Magic Ingredient

What gives bread its delicious flavor and distinctive, chewy texture? Long ago, human beings learned that if they placed a mixture of flour, honey, and water near an open window on a warm day, something mysterious would happen. The ball of dough would grow until it had doubled in size.

What made the dough rise? To our ancestors, the process must have seemed like magic. In fact, objects too small to see had floated in on the breeze and landed on the flour mixture. Tiny spores of a living substance called yeast fed on the other ingredients and began to form carbon dioxide, which created bubbles within the dough. The bubbles made the dough expand.

Take a quick look at both passages and the questions so you know what to expect.

What is this passage mostly about? Look at the subheads.

What makes bread so good?

Today you don't have to wait for yeast to float in your window in order to bake a loaf of bread. You can buy it in the grocery store. Be sure to check the expiration date marked on the outside of the packet. To make sure the yeast is still active, you can follow a process called proofing. Put some lukewarm water and a little sugar in a bowl and sprinkle in the yeast. If bubbles form, that proves the yeast is working.

Yeast is not the only leavening agent used to make bread, although it is the most common. Irish soda bread is made with baking soda. Banana bread, corn bread, and zucchini bread are usually leavened with baking powder. However, all of the traditional breads that people use for toast and sandwiches contain yeast.

Flour

The second essential ingredient in bread is wheat. Wheat is a grain, or seedlike plant. In the Stone Age, people pounded wheat between stones to make it edible. Today, it is milled into the powdery stuff we know as flour. A single grain of wheat makes thousands of flour particles!

In whole wheat flour, all of the parts of the grain are included. When making white flour, the seed coats are removed. White bread used to be more expensive, and only rich people could afford it. But the brown bread that poor people ate was much better for them because it contained more nutrients.

Wheat is not the only grain used to make bread. Rye, barley, and other grains are also used. However, wheat contains a special protein called gluten, which is stretchy. It allows wheat flour to stretch and contain the gas bubbles produced by yeast.

Kinds of Bread

Different countries have different favorite breads. Pumpernickel, which contains a mixture of wheat flour, rye flour, cornmeal, and caraway seeds, is popular in Germany, Russia, and Sweden.

Challah is traditional Jewish bread made with eggs and braided into different shapes. Portuguese sweet bread is also made with eggs, but it has much more sugar than does challah.

The famous long, thin loaf known as French bread is actually from Austria, not France! True French bread comes in a round loaf.

Hungary and Norway have traditional breads that contain grated or mashed potatoes as well as flour. The potatoes give the bread a wonderfully moist texture and a delicious taste.

Think about how this passage is organized.

Standardized Test Tutor: Reading (Grade 5) © 2009 by Michael Priestley, Scholastic Teaching Resources

Passage 2: Oatmeal Bread

Ingredients

3 cups boiling water

2 cups coarse rolled oats

1 teaspoon sugar

2 packages active dry yeast

$\frac{1}{2}$ cup warm water

1 tablespoon salt

$\frac{1}{3}$ cup molasses

2 tablespoons butter

$6\frac{1}{2}$ cups unbleached flour

> What kind of passage is this?

Directions

1. Pour the boiling water over the oats to cook them and then put them aside to cool.
2. Mix sugar and yeast in the warm water and allow to proof.
3. Stir the cooled oats, salt, molasses, and butter together.
4. Add the proofed yeast to the rest of the ingredients.
5. Stir in the flour, one cup at a time.
6. Turn the mixture onto a floured board and knead for about 10 minutes until elastic, adding extra flour if needed.
7. Place the dough in a buttered bowl and then cover until it has doubled in size.
8. Knead the dough a second time.
9. Divide in two and place into buttered bread tins.
10. Bake at 375 degrees for 50 minutes, until finished. (Loaves should be golden brown and sound hollow when tapped.)

Diagnosing Problem Bread

If a loaf of bread is less than perfect, you may have one of the following problems:

Problem	Reason
Too damp	Bread did not cook long enough.
Top of loaf sags in the middle	Dough was not kneaded enough.
Large holes in the bread	Dough rose too long.
Dough contains small, hard lumps	Dough was not mixed enough at first.
Loaf rose more on one side than the other	Loaf was not placed in center of oven to bake.

> What kind of information does this chart give you?

Questions 33–40: Choose the best answer to each question.

For each question, decide which passage it refers to.

33. Passage 1 says, "Yeast is not the only *leavening* agent used to make bread." What is a *leavening* agent?

   Ⓐ a type of bread

   Ⓑ a machine used to turn grain into flour

   Ⓒ a kind of gas

   Ⓓ a substance that makes dough rise

Go back to the second section of Passage 1 to find the answer.

34. Which detail best supports the idea that bread has long been a very important food for all kinds of people?

   Ⓐ Archaeologists have found bread in Egyptian tombs.

   Ⓑ In ancient Greece, bakers argued about their bread.

   Ⓒ During the Middle Ages, strict laws controlled the price of bread.

   Ⓓ In England, some people brought their dough to a public bake house.

Look for the answer in the first two paragraphs of Passage 1.

35. In Passage 1, what is the main idea of the section called **The Magic Ingredient**?

   Ⓐ Yeast is the substance that gives bread its special texture.

   Ⓑ Before people understood science, they believed in magic.

   Ⓒ Using yeast, you can make water bubble and expand.

   Ⓓ Wheat flour contains an amazing ingredient called gluten.

Decide what this section is mostly about.

36. When making oatmeal bread, what should you do before you combine the molasses and the oats?

   Ⓐ Add the yeast to the molasses.

   Ⓑ Cook the oats.

   Ⓒ Add the flour to the oats.

   Ⓓ Knead the dough.

Review the directions in Passage 2. Pay attention to the order of the steps.

37. Passage 2 mainly tells about—

Ⓐ different types of oatmeal bread and where they are made.

Ⓑ what you need to make oatmeal bread and how to bake it correctly.

Ⓒ all of the things that can go wrong when you bake oatmeal bread.

Ⓓ how oats are grown and milled to make oatmeal.

> Think about the purpose of this passage.

38. Which sentence from Passage 1 states an opinion?

Ⓐ In ancient Rome, bakers enjoyed special privileges because their bread was so valued.

Ⓑ In 1327, some dishonest bakers made secret openings in the counters where the loaves were placed.

Ⓒ The brown bread that poor people ate was much better for them because it contained more nutrients.

Ⓓ The potatoes give the bread a wonderfully moist texture and a delicious taste.

> Choose the sentence that cannot be verified as fact.

39. According to the chart showing common problems with bread, what can happen if dough rises too long?

Ⓐ There will be large holes in the bread.

Ⓑ The bread will be damp.

Ⓒ There will be small, hard lumps in the bread.

Ⓓ The bread will look uneven.

> Go back to the chart to find the answer.

40. In addition to the information in these two passages, which personal experience would a reader need in order to make a loaf of bread?

Ⓐ knowing how to proof yeast

Ⓑ knowing how to cook oats

Ⓒ knowing when a loaf is finished

Ⓓ knowing how to knead dough

> Look for the topic that is *not* explained in the passages.

End of Test 1 **STOP**

Read each passage and the questions that follow. Look at the Test Tutor's tips for understanding the passages and answering the questions. Then choose the best answer to each question.

Directions: Read this passage about some unusual living things. Then answer questions 1–5.

Fungi

Every living thing on Earth is either a plant or an animal, right? Wrong! Many organisms in our world are neither. Some of these mysterious inhabitants float invisibly through the air, and some lie hidden in the ground. They do not need sunlight to survive, and if the weather becomes too cold, they can become dormant until conditions improve.

What are these creatures? They are called fungi, and you see them almost every day. Many kinds of fungi seem disgusting, such as the yucky green and moldy black stuff that sprouts on food left too long in the refrigerator. But other kinds are not so bad. For example, the yeast that bakers use to make bread rise is a type of fungus. Mushrooms are also fungi.

Special Features

What makes fungi different from plants and animals? An animal can move around independently. Fungi get around too, but they don't have feet, wings, or tails. They have to wait for wind or some other outside force to move them. Plants are different from fungi because they contain a substance called chlorophyll. It helps them make food from the energy in sunlight. Fungi do not contain chlorophyll.

> Take a quick look at the questions before you begin reading.

> Find the main idea of this section by reading the first sentence.

Standardized Test Tutor: Reading (Grade 5) © 2009 by Michael Priestley, Scholastic Teaching Resources

Harmful or Beneficial?

Some fungi are harmful, while others are beneficial. Some fungi cause diseases, such as athlete's foot, which makes feet itchy. Other fungi, such as molds, are useful. They are used to make penicillin and other antibiotics, which have saved countless lives. Drugs like these are used to cure nasty infections and other diseases.

Antibiotics Timeline

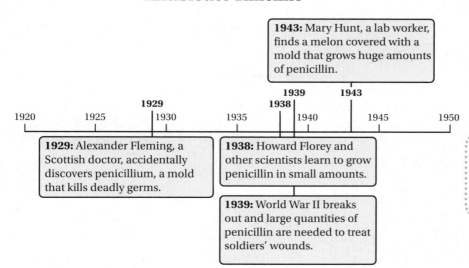

1943: Mary Hunt, a lab worker, finds a melon covered with a mold that grows huge amounts of penicillin.

1920   1925   **1929**   1935   **1939**   1945   1950
                  1930   **1938** 1940   **1943**

1929: Alexander Fleming, a Scottish doctor, accidentally discovers penicillium, a mold that kills deadly germs.

1938: Howard Florey and other scientists learn to grow penicillin in small amounts.

1939: World War II breaks out and large quantities of penicillin are needed to treat soldiers' wounds.

> This is a subhead. How does it help you?

> Look at the timeline. Why does the author include this?

Nature's Recyclers

Fungi clean up more than germs and wounds, though. They are the world's first recyclers. Without fungi, our world would be a mess. Since fungi cannot make their own food as plants do, they must get their food elsewhere. Many fungi get their nutrients from dead plants, such as old, dead leaves. In the process, they break down these dead plants and turn them into soil. The fungi get a meal, and the world gets a housecleaning!

Questions 1–5: Choose the best answer to each question.

1. Read this sentence from the passage.

    They do not need sunlight to survive, and if the weather becomes too cold, they can become *dormant* until conditions improve.

    Being *dormant* is most like—

    Ⓐ taking a trip.

    Ⓑ eating food.

    Ⓒ finding shelter.

    Ⓓ falling asleep.

Go back to the first paragraph to see how the word is used.

2. What is the section called **Special Features** mostly about?

    Ⓐ what fungi look like

    Ⓑ how fungi are different from plants and animals

    Ⓒ some of the ways that humans use fungi

    Ⓓ when different types of fungi were discovered

Go back to the passage and review this section.

3. The author most likely wrote this passage to—

    Ⓐ help readers recognize fungi in the wild.

    Ⓑ tell an entertaining story about people and fungi.

    Ⓒ give information about fungi.

    Ⓓ compare mushrooms with other kinds of fungi.

Think about the purpose of the passage as a whole.

4. Which sentence states an opinion?

    Ⓐ They are called fungi, and you see them almost every day.

    Ⓑ Many kinds of fungi seem disgusting.

    Ⓒ Some fungi cause diseases, such as athlete's foot, which makes feet itchy.

    Ⓓ The fungi get a meal, and the world gets a housecleaning.

Look for a statement that cannot be proven true.

5. Why don't fungi need sunlight to survive?

    Ⓐ They do not have chlorophyll.

    Ⓑ They can become dormant.

    Ⓒ They do not move independently.

    Ⓓ They can float through the air.

Read all of the answer choices carefully. Look for one that is related to sunlight.

Standardized Test Tutor: Reading (Grade 5) © 2009 by Michael Priestley, Scholastic Teaching Resources

Directions: Read this passage based on a story from the Mayan people of Mexico. Then answer questions 6–11.

The First Music

When the gods created Earth, they made it a living thing, with a beating heart at its center. Then they covered its surface with people and with many wonderful things for the people to use. They gave the people water to drink and corn to eat. They gave them fire so they could warm themselves and wind so they could cool themselves. They gave them trees for fuel and shelter, tall mountains to climb, golden sunlight for work and play, and hours of darkness for sleep.

> Look for details that tell where the story takes place.

Yet still something was missing. The gods watched the people carefully to see what it was. The people were strong and healthy, but their steps were slow and their faces were often melancholy. They never lifted their voices in song or swayed their bodies in dance. The gods had forgotten to give the world the gift of music!

The gods gathered together under the Tree of Life to hold a council about this problem, and one of them, Ah Kin Xooc, spoke up.

"Each of you must give me a sound."

The gods eagerly agreed. The God of Corn said, "I give you the soft rustle of the leaves of corn when the breeze stirs them."

> Think about what the characters say and do.

The God of Water said, "I will provide the babble of a brook, the crash of ocean waves, the lapping of a lake, and the patter of raindrops."

From others, Ah Kin Xooc gathered the calls of birds and animals, the sizzle and pop of fire, and the eerie sounds of night.

Then, to the surprise of the other gods, Ah Kin Xooc took all of the sounds he had been given and swallowed them!

Ah Kin Xooc made his way to the center of Earth, where the heart beat steady and strong. Opening his mouth, he let out all of the sounds, and their melodies mixed with the rhythm of the heartbeat. The music rose to the surface of Earth like bubbles rising to the surface of a lake and spread far and wide, and the people listened in amazement.

> Think about how the people have changed.

From that moment on, the people had music to help express their deepest feelings. When they were sad, they mourned with slow, deep notes. When they were joyous, they played pounding rhythms on drums and wild melodies on flutes and leaped high in the air. Ah Kin Xooc had given them the greatest gift of all.

Standardized Test Tutor: Reading (Grade 5) © 2009 by Michael Priestley, Scholastic Teaching Resources

Questions 6–11: Choose the best answer to each question.

6. You can tell that this passage is a myth because it—

   Ⓐ uses dialogue to show what the characters are thinking.

   Ⓑ describes how the world was created by gods.

   Ⓒ focuses on the solution to a difficult problem.

   Ⓓ takes place in a mysterious setting.

> Find the answer that is true only of myths and not of other genres.

7. In this story, music rising through Earth is compared to—

   Ⓐ bubbles in a lake.

   Ⓑ a person's heartbeat.

   Ⓒ the crash of waves.

   Ⓓ water dripping on a roof.

> Look at the ending of the story to find the answer.

8. What was the problem in this story?

   Ⓐ The people did not appreciate all of the gifts from the gods.

   Ⓑ The gods forgot to give Earth a living heart.

   Ⓒ The people were sad because they could not be gods.

   Ⓓ The gods forgot to give people a way to express their feelings.

> Go back to the beginning of the story to find the answer.

9. Read this sentence from the story.

   The people were strong and healthy, but their steps were slow and their faces were often *melancholy*.

   What is the meaning of the word *melancholy*?

   Ⓐ angry

   Ⓑ thin

   Ⓒ sad

   Ⓓ forgetful

> Look for clues in the sentences before and after this word.

Standardized Test Tutor: Reading (Grade 5) © 2009 by Michael Priestley, Scholastic Teaching Resources

10. What happened immediately after Ah Kin Xooc let the sounds out of his mouth?

Ⓐ The other gods listened to the sounds.

Ⓑ The sounds mixed with Earth's heartbeat.

Ⓒ The sounds covered Earth.

Ⓓ People turned the sounds into songs.

> Go back to this part of the story to find the answer.

11. What is the main theme of this story?

Ⓐ People need to depend on one another for survival.

Ⓑ Great musicians are different from ordinary people.

Ⓒ Nature can be terribly cruel or wonderfully kind.

Ⓓ People need more than food and shelter to be happy.

> Think about the lesson you can learn from what happens.

Directions: Read this poem about a father and son. Then answer questions 12–17.

Seeing the Moon

"Get your jacket," urges my father,
"The heavy one with the hood—
It's freezing outside."

"I think I'll just stay in," I answer, avoiding his eyes.
"It's almost time for me to go to bed."   5

"You can stay up late for this," he says, as if it's some big treat.
Can't he see I'm not interested?

His glasses are fogging up in the warm kitchen,
But behind the blurry disks, his eyes get big and surprised.
He can't believe I mean it!   10

"Come on, Josh, you'll love it!" he insists.
"I have the telescope all set up!"

"Okay," I sigh, and shuffle to the closet in my slippers,
Like Grandpa on a rainy day,
But Dad doesn't notice.   15
He rubs his hands with excitement.

Outside, I crane my neck.
A cloud covers the moon, but
"Just wait!" says my dad.
Sure enough, the blanket drops away,   20
Revealing a strange sight:
The moon, turned dusky red.

I put my eye to the telescope.
Blink.
Adjust the focus.   25
Search.

And there it is!
No longer a flat, white coin in the sky,
But a rusty sphere,
With big blotches of brown,   30
So real and round,
The moon
Staring calmly back at me.

Who are the main characters in this poem?

What are the main characters doing?

That's when I realize
That it is all real: 35
The moon, the sun, the stars, the galaxies, the universe, and all . . .
Not just a pretty cutout hanging over my world,
But a series of real worlds,
World after world after world . . .

I feel dizzy and pull away from the eyepiece.   40
My dad is looking at me, and smiling in a different way.
He says nothing,
And that's when I realize that he sees me,
And I see him.
We're both real, not just cutouts in each other's lives.   45

He takes his turn at the telescope.
It's very cold.
We say good night to the big red moon
And go inside for something hot to drink.

—*Stacey Sparks*

What change has taken place?

Questions 12–17: Choose the best answer to each question.

12. Which line from the poem contains an example of personification?

Ⓐ But behind the blurry disks, his eyes get big and surprised.

Ⓑ Sure enough, the blanket drops away,

Ⓒ No longer a flat, white coin in the sky,

Ⓓ The moon staring calmly back at me.

Read each answer choice before you pick one.

13. Where are the father and son at the beginning of this poem?

Ⓐ outside a school

Ⓑ in a kitchen

Ⓒ at a science museum

Ⓓ in their backyard

Go back to the beginning of the poem to find the answer.

14. How is the father different at the end of the poem from in the beginning?

Ⓐ He realizes that the lunar eclipse is not really important.

Ⓑ He is sorry that he forced his son to come outside.

Ⓒ He understands what his son is feeling.

Ⓓ He believes that someday he and his son will get along better.

Read the ending again.

15. Most of the images and descriptive words in this poem are related to—

Ⓐ sight.

Ⓑ sound.

Ⓒ heat.

Ⓓ love.

Scan the poem to see what kinds of words are used.

16. Which line from the poem contains alliteration?

Ⓐ His glasses are fogging up in the warm kitchen,

Ⓑ Like Grandpa on a rainy day,

Ⓒ The moon, turned dusky red.

Ⓓ With big blotches of brown,

Think about what alliteration means, then read all of the answer choices carefully.

17. Read these lines from the poem.

> Not just a pretty cutout hanging over my world,
> But a series of real worlds,
> World after world after world . . .

The speaker repeats the word *world* in these lines in order to—

Ⓐ show that he is getting upset.

Ⓑ demonstrate the size of the universe.

Ⓒ create a series of rhymes.

Ⓓ stress how tired he is becoming.

Read this part of the poem again.

Standardized Test Tutor: Reading (Grade 5) © 2009 by Michael Priestley, Scholastic Teaching Resources

Directions: Read this passage from a school newspaper. Then answer questions 18–24.

From the *Darnell Elementary School Eagle*

Editorial

Recently, our school cut the length of recess down from 30 minutes a day to 20 minutes. This is terrible! My friends and I like to make up different games to play at recess. It takes a few minutes just to figure out what we want to play and divide into teams. How can we finish a whole game in just 15 minutes?

I have a better idea. How about making recess longer instead of shorter? Originally, I was going to propose lengthening recess to 45 minutes. However, after conducting careful research on the Internet, I have an even better suggestion. Let's make recess two hours—every day!

I don't want a two-hour recess because I am lazy or just want to fool around. No, I have found many scientific reasons to back my proposal.

1. Studies show that people learn better when they have a break once in a while. Studying takes a lot of hard work and concentration. After a while, your brain just gets tired. I figure if a short break helps you focus better, then a long one will help even more. If Darnell Elementary adopts my two-hour-recess policy, I bet all of us kids will turn into geniuses!

2. Kids don't have as much time to play together as they used to. Our parents and teachers are always telling us about how when they were little, they ran around outside for hours every day. Our parents won't let us do that! They make us stay in the yard or in the apartment after school. Isn't that sad? If we had two hours of recess, we could learn all of the cool games our parents played when they were kids: kick the can, capture the flag, stickball, and all of those complicated jump-rope moves. We would have more to talk to our parents about, too!

3. Recess is one of the few times when kids have "unstructured" activity. This means they can do whatever they want, from playing tag to just sitting on a log. In class, the teachers tell us what to do. After school, we have organized sports and lessons. How are we ever going to grow up and become leaders if we don't get more practice making decisions? When recess is only 20 minutes long, there's no time to figure out if we were smart and thought up a good new game. The game is over as soon as it starts. With a two-hour recess, we could tell

Standardized Test Tutor: Reading (Grade 5) © 2009 by Michael Priestley, Scholastic Teaching Resources

which kids were good planners and good thinkers. The kids who weren't so good at first would have time to get better. A two-hour recess is definitely the answer to building great leaders for our country's future!

4. Everyone is nagging kids about our health. They tell us that we watch too much TV. They complain that we play too many electronic games. They criticize us for spending hours in front of the computer. They also say we eat too much fast food.

Well, I have a great answer to this problem. Where's the one place where there are no TVs or computers or fast-food restaurants? You guessed it: the playground! Under my recess proposal, kids would be guaranteed hours each day where they had to be active and creative instead of couch potatoes. We could turn into a nation of superheroes! Our legs would be like steel from running and jumping. Our arms would be like iron from swinging on the monkey bars. Probably no one would even need glasses anymore because they wouldn't wear out their vision staring at a computer screen!

5. Some people will probably say that the school day is not long enough for a two-hour recess. They will say that we need to spend all of our time on reading, math, writing, science, and social studies. I say that a two-hour recess will teach skills that will help us in ALL our other subjects. Learning counting-out and jump-rope rhymes is kind of like memorizing poetry, so it will help us with reading. Keeping score is a math skill. Being outside, we will see a lot of birds and bugs and worms, which is science. Finally, learning how kids get along in groups is part of social studies. I haven't figured out how recess helps with writing, but with my new, high-powered two-hour recess brain, I probably will!

Fellow Darnell Elementary students: Help me spread the word of my great plan. Talk to your teachers, talk to your parents, and talk to your neighbors. If they think it's a silly idea, be sure to tell them all of my great reasons and how I researched them. If grown-ups get tired of you talking so much about this topic, just say, "I probably would be a little calmer and less obnoxious if I had two-hour recess every day!"

Think about why this passage was written.

Questions 18–24: Choose the best answer to each question.

18. The passage says, "Originally, I was going to *propose* lengthening recess to 45 minutes." Which definition of *propose* best fits in this sentence?

> **propose** *verb* **1.** to suggest an idea. **2.** to make an offer of marriage. **3.** to plan or intend. **4.** to nominate a person for office.

(A) definition 1

(B) definition 2

(C) definition 3

(D) definition 4

> Try each definition in the sentence before you choose.

19. How is most of the information in this passage organized?

(A) A number of events are presented in chronological order.

(B) An argument is presented, followed by the opposite argument.

(C) A solution is presented, followed by support.

(D) An event is described, followed by its causes.

> Skim the passage again to see how it is organized.

20. According to the writer, what is one effect of unstructured activity?

(A) It helps people concentrate better.

(B) It teaches decision-making skills.

(C) It makes kids more calm and polite.

(D) It helps kids get stronger.

> Go back to this section in the passage.

21. What is the main idea of point 2 in the editorial?

(A) Kids and their parents need to spend more time together.

(B) Kids can't play together as easily as their parents used to.

(C) Parents make their kids stay too close to home.

(D) The world today is a dangerous place.

> Find the sentence that tells what this part is mostly about.

22. The writer of this editorial includes the reference to doing research on the Internet to—

Ⓐ show how many kids today are "couch potatoes."

Ⓑ demonstrate that he is not lazy.

Ⓒ support his idea to have a longer recess.

Ⓓ explain why kids can't take breaks from classes.

Scan the passage to find what the author says about the Internet.

23. Which detail in the editorial is *least* essential to the author's argument?

Ⓐ If we had two hours of recess, we could learn all of the cool games our parents played.

Ⓑ Everyone is nagging kids about our health.

Ⓒ Keeping score is a math skill.

Ⓓ I haven't figured out how recess helps with writing.

Notice the word *least* in the question.

24. Which is the best summary of this editorial?

Ⓐ Schools all over the country are cutting the numbers of minutes in recess.

Ⓑ Making recess longer would make kids smarter, stronger, and better leaders.

Ⓒ The playground is a place where there are no computers, televisions, or fast-food restaurants.

Ⓓ Life is very different for kids today than it was for their parents and teachers.

Look for the summary that tells about the whole passage.

Standardized Test Tutor: Reading (Grade 5) © 2009 by Michael Priestley, Scholastic Teaching Resources

Directions: Read this passage about a girl who goes to summer camp. Then answer questions 25–32.

Summer Camp

Ketia pulled her Camp Bluetooth T-shirt over her head and started lacing up her sneakers. Aunt Marjorie stood proudly by, beaming as if Ketia had just achieved something amazing.

"Why exactly is it called Camp Bluetooth?" asked Ketia as she applied mosquito repellent to her arms and legs.

Aunt Marjorie sighed. "You asked me that before, Ketia. The camp is named after the beautiful mountains that rise in the distance. They are jagged, like teeth, and they look blue because they are so far away."

Ketia thought that jagged blue teeth sounded terrible, but she didn't want to hurt Aunt Marjorie's feelings. Aunt Marjorie loved Camp Bluetooth. She and Ketia's mother had attended the camp every summer when they were girls, and she had offered to pay for Ketia to fly all the way from Wisconsin to North Carolina to go to the camp for two weeks this summer. If Ketia had been given the choice between tramping around a nature camp for two weeks with a bunch of strangers or hanging out at the municipal pool back home with her friends, she would have stayed at home. But no one had given her the choice. Her mother and aunt had just assumed she would jump at the chance to go to Camp Bluetooth, and she didn't want to disappoint them.

"Now, let's make sure you have everything," said Aunt Marjorie. She checked the official list from the camp. "Hat, sunscreen, rain poncho, bathing suit, plain white T-shirt, towel, water bottle, packed lunch, backpack."

Ketia nodded glumly. The pack was heavy. Not only was she going to be lonely and bored, but she was going to have a sore back from hauling all her stuff through the woods.

For the first time since picking Ketia up at the airport, Aunt Marjorie's big smile wavered and almost disappeared. "Nothing's wrong, is it, Ketia?"

"No," said Ketia, trying to remember how to smile herself. "Let's go!"

They drove for about fifteen minutes, and then Aunt Marjorie pulled down a dirt road. It was so narrow that every time they met a car coming the other direction, Aunt Marjorie had to pull over so the car could pass. Instead of acting grumpy, Aunt Marjorie kept waving.

Look for details that tell about the setting and the characters.

Think about the problem or conflict in this story.

"I think that was Faye Morgan (or Luella Pease or Jane Anne Simmons)!" she would say. "I think she was at camp with your mother and me!"

Finally, they reached a parking area next to a big field. Kids were everywhere—little kids clinging to their parents' hands, older ones playing tag and Frisbee. Ketia slowly got out of the car. She felt shy and awkward. What if she couldn't find her group?

In the middle of the field, a tall counselor wearing a tie-dyed shirt was playing tag with a group of kids about Ketia's age.

To Ketia's amazement, the counselor said, "Ketia, right? Awesome. That means we're all here. Ketia, my name is Nellie, and I'm here to welcome you to the greatest camp ever."

The rest of the day went by in a blur. The morning was spent on a hike through the woods. Nellie seemed to know the name of every tree and creature that they passed. She showed the campers how to recognize birds by their songs as well as by sight. She also knew verse after verse of camp songs, which she proceeded to teach her group.

Lunch was at picnic tables beside a beautiful lake. After a rest, the campers were all tested and put into groups according to how well they could swim. When Ketia tested into the top group, Nellie yelled, "Hey, give me five!" and slapped Ketia's hand. Ketia realized that swimming in the lake was even better than swimming in the pool at home, and her whole feeling about the next two weeks changed.

After the swim, Nellie's group headed to the Craft Cabin. Nellie told everyone to take out their plain white T-shirt, and then she handed around rubber bands. "We're going to tie-dye these boring T-shirts so everyone can have one that's as awesome as mine!"

At 3:30, ten rainbow shirts hung on the clothesline outside the cabin, and ten exhausted campers were heading back to the field. Ketia's damp bathing suit had soaked through her backpack, she had a blister on her left little toe, and her backpack straps were digging into her shoulders.

"Say 'So long' to your fellow campers," ordered Nellie. "They're going to be your best friends by the end of two weeks, and you'll probably be back next year. That's just how it goes around here!"

Ketia grinned. Then she staggered toward Aunt Marjorie's car. Her aunt wore a worried frown on her face as she watched Ketia approach—until Ketia gave the thumbs-up sign. "It's all good, Aunt Marjorie!" she said.

Think about what the characters do and say in the end.

Standardized Test Tutor: Reading (Grade 5) © 2009 by Michael Priestley, Scholastic Teaching Resources

Questions 25–32: Choose the best answer to each question.

25. The passage says that Ketia applied *mosquito repellent* to her arms and legs. What is *mosquito repellent*?

Ⓐ something that keeps mosquitoes off

Ⓑ someone who studies mosquitoes

Ⓒ something that soothes the itch from mosquito bites

Ⓓ something that traps mosquitoes

> Look at the parts of the word to figure out what it means.

26. Why does Ketia decide to go to Camp Bluetooth?

Ⓐ She has heard that kids love it so much they return every year.

Ⓑ She thinks she will be bored if she stays at home all summer.

Ⓒ She wants to make her mother and her aunt happy.

Ⓓ She has always wanted to explore North Carolina.

> Go back to the beginning of the story to find the answer.

27. How does the setting of this story affect the events?

Ⓐ The main character learns important family truths by visiting her aunt's hometown.

Ⓑ The main character experiences a conflict between the values she has learned growing up and the values in a new setting.

Ⓒ The main character experiences a number of humorous misunderstandings based on the challenges of a new environment.

Ⓓ The main character has an interesting new experience in a setting far from home.

> Think of what would change in a different setting.

28. Which behavior shows that Aunt Marjorie is aware of how other people feel?

Ⓐ She sighs when Ketia asks about the name of the camp.

Ⓑ She offers to pay for Ketia to fly to North Carolina.

Ⓒ She keeps waving in excitement at passing cars.

Ⓓ She worriedly frowns at Ketia at the end of the day.

> You can learn about a character from what she says and does.

29. Which event represents the most important turning point in Ketia's feelings about going to camp?

Ⓐ being welcomed by Nellie

Ⓑ learning camp songs .

Ⓒ swimming in the lake

Ⓓ tie-dyeing a T-shirt

> Compare all of the answer choices before you pick one. Go back to the story if necessary.

30. Which word best describes Nellie?

Ⓐ cheerful

Ⓑ strict

Ⓒ calm

Ⓓ artistic

> Imagine Nellie as a real person. What is she like?

31. Which experience would best help a reader understand Ketia's feelings?

Ⓐ entering a swimming competition

Ⓑ spending a holiday with cousins

Ⓒ working on a project in art class

Ⓓ starting at a new school

> Choose the one that makes the most sense to you.

32. Which of Ketia's expectations of her first day at camp turns out to be true?

Ⓐ She will be lonely.

Ⓑ She will get sore from carrying her stuff.

Ⓒ She will be bored.

Ⓓ She will have trouble finding her group.

> Think about how Ketia feels at the end.

Standardized Test Tutor: Reading (Grade 5) © 2009 by Michael Priestley, Scholastic Teaching Resources

Directions: Read these two passages about chimpanzees and a person who studies them. Then answer questions 33–40.

Passage 1: Jane Goodall

Jane Goodall is one of the world's most famous primatologists, or scientists who study apes and monkeys. For decades, Goodall lived mostly in Tanzania in East Africa, observing chimpanzees in the wild.

As a young child, Jane Goodall was fascinated by animals. She grew up in the English countryside and was always climbing trees or riding horses. She and her friends spent hours racing snails in the garden!

In some ways, Jane was always unusual. When she was 5 years old, she disappeared for hours. Her mother was just about to call the police when Jane showed up! She had been curious about how chickens lay eggs. She had followed a hen into the henhouse, but the hen got frightened and ran away. Jane did not give up. She decided to wait quietly for another hen to show up. She had to wait for a long time. Finally a hen arrived, and she got to see it lay an egg.

Jane also had a powerful imagination. One of her favorite characters was Dr. Dolittle, a doctor who traveled to Africa and spoke to the animals. Jane read *The Story of Dr. Dolittle* when she was 7 and decided to go to Africa someday. Many children of her time probably had the same dream but then forgot it. Jane never forgot.

Jane also loved horses and frequently rode when she was young. Later, when she couldn't afford to ride as much as she wanted, Jane found ways to make herself useful to the owner of a local riding stable. She washed saddles. She groomed and fed ponies. Eventually, she took customers out for rides. She was always willing to speak up and work hard for what she wanted.

The animal Jane loved most as a girl was a dog named Rusty. He wasn't hers; he belonged to a neighbor. Rusty was very clever, and Jane used to teach him tricks. By watching Rusty carefully, Jane learned a lot about animals. She learned that they can remember things. They can solve simple problems. They have feelings.

Skim both passages and the questions before you begin reading.

Who is Jane Goodall, and what did she do?

When Jane was in her early twenties, she finally got a chance to go to Africa. Even though she had never been to college, she got a job with a famous scientist named Louis Leakey. Leakey and his wife, Mary, were looking for fossils in a remote part of Tanzania. Jane helped them, but the most exciting part of her new job was being surrounded by wild animals: lions, hyenas, and rhinos.

Jane dreamed of learning how animals communicate, like Dr. Dolittle. One day Louis Leakey said he needed a volunteer. He wanted someone to go to a remote lake in Tanzania to study a band of chimpanzees there. Jane was thrilled.

On July 16, 1960, she set up her tent in what is now known as Gombe National Park. Then she began to explore. At first, the chimps ran away from Jane. But gradually, they got used to her presence.

Over the years, Jane got to know the individual members of the chimpanzee band who lived in Gombe. Every day, from sunrise to sunset, she would follow them through the park, taking notes on their behavior. She learned many new things about these intelligent creatures. She observed one chimp strip the leaves off a twig, dip it into a hole in the ground, and pull out some termites to eat. Before this, no one knew that animals could make tools.

She learned how some chimps became good leaders. She watched how mother chimpanzees raised their children. She watched animals get angry and get sad. She wrote everything down so others would understand animals as she did. Like Dr. Dolittle, she learned that if you pay really close attention to animals, you will understand what they are "saying."

Passage 2: Chimpanzees

A chimpanzee is a primate. This group includes tiny bush babies, monkeys, apes, and humans. Full-grown chimps are 4 to 5 feet tall. The males weigh about 100 pounds, while the females weigh 90 pounds or less. Chimpanzees have long fingers and toes, and they are covered with dark fur except on their faces, which are very expressive.

Chimpanzee Habitat
Chimpanzees live in western and central Africa, near the equator. Some chimps live in dense rain forests. Others live in thinner woodland.

> How does this passage connect to Passage 1?

Standardized Test Tutor: Reading (Grade 5) © 2009 by Michael Priestley, Scholastic Teaching Resources

Chimps usually walk on all four legs, but they can also walk upright. Chimps are good climbers, and they can swing through trees. They usually sleep in trees at night.

Chimpanzee Behavior

Chimps live in groups, called communities, which may contain up to 80 members. Within each community are many smaller groups of friends and family members. Young chimps stay with their mothers until they are about 8 years old.

Just like human beings who live and work in groups, some chimps are more powerful than others. Getting a high rank depends on more than size. Group leaders are usually strong-willed and clever.

Chimps often "argue" over food or to protect their children. Most quarrels end quickly, but sometimes chimps get hurt. Chimpanzees are powerful animals, and they will bite and kick if angry.

Chimpanzees eat fruits, plants, insects, eggs, and small animals. They use twigs to "fish" inside insect nests for food. They use leaves to soak up water to drink. They also use stones to crack open nutshells.

Chimpanzee Communication

Chimpanzees communicate with their voices. They screech, hoot, and howl to show anger, fear, and other emotions. They warn each other when enemies are near. Chimps also communicate with gestures and facial expressions. If a chimp holds out its hand, it is begging for food. A hug means "Hello" or "I'm scared." Some chimps have even learned to use sign language.

Questions 33–40: Choose the best answer to each question.

33. What is the main idea of Passage 1?

Ⓐ People do not need to go to college or university to become great scientists.

Ⓑ Jane Goodall learned how hens lay eggs and taught a dog to do tricks.

Ⓒ Chimpanzees, like all animals, have their own special system of communication.

Ⓓ Jane Goodall was fascinated by animals and spent much of her life studying chimpanzees in the wild.

> Check all of the answer choices before you pick one.

34. Which detail supports the idea that Jane was always willing to work hard for what she wanted?

Ⓐ She wanted to be like Dr. Dolittle and talk to animals.

Ⓑ She went to Africa when she was in her early twenties.

Ⓒ She got a job with a famous scientist named Louis Leakey.

Ⓓ She loved being surrounded by hyenas, lions, and rhinos.

> Look for the choice that is related to working.

35. Which animal first taught Jane that she had to be patient in order to understand it?

Ⓐ a horse

Ⓑ a hen

Ⓒ a dog

Ⓓ a snail

> Review the passage to find the answer.

36. What is the most likely reason Jane Goodall stopped looking for fossils with Louis Leakey and his wife?

Ⓐ She got lonely working in such a remote place.

Ⓑ She could not take advice from an older person.

Ⓒ She was afraid of the lions and rhinos.

Ⓓ She wanted to focus on living creatures.

> Find the reason that is supported by information in the passage.

Standardized Test Tutor: Reading (Grade 5) © 2009 by Michael Priestley, Scholastic Teaching Resources

37. In Passage 2, the purpose of the headings is to—

Ⓐ help the reader quickly find information about chimpanzees.

Ⓑ capture the reader's interest with clever sayings.

Ⓒ sum up important scientific discoveries about chimpanzees.

Ⓓ encourage the reader to ask questions about chimpanzees.

> Think about why the author uses headings.

38. Which sentence best summarizes the section called **Chimpanzee Communication** in Passage 2?

Ⓐ Chimpanzees can communicate in many ways.

Ⓑ Chimpanzees express feelings with their voices.

Ⓒ Chimpanzees have feelings such as anger and fear.

Ⓓ Chimpanzees learn to communicate from their mothers.

> Go back to this part of the passage.

39. According to Passage 2, what is one way that chimpanzees are like humans?

Ⓐ Some individuals use tools, but others do not.

Ⓑ Some chimpanzees live in large groups, and some live alone.

Ⓒ Some members of a community have a higher rank than others.

Ⓓ Young chimpanzees stay with their mothers until the age of 8.

> Scan the passage to see where humans are mentioned.

40. Both of these passages emphasize the idea that—

Ⓐ Jane Goodall was a famous scientist who studied chimpanzees.

Ⓑ chimpanzees are fascinating and highly intelligent.

Ⓒ Jane Goodall liked to record scientific information and observations.

Ⓓ chimpanzees live in western and central Africa, near the equator.

> Find the idea that applies to both passages, not just one.

End of Test 2 STOP

Good Luck!

Directions: Read this passage about a storyteller. Then answer questions 1–5.

Kasim's Lesson

Once there was a storyteller named Kasim who lived in Tashkent, in central Asia. Tashkent was a city where travelers from many countries crossed paths. In the evenings, when their work was done, these travelers far from home sought entertainment. They loved stories, the wilder the better. Of all the storytellers, Kasim became most famous for his extravagant tall tales.

At first Kasim, like all great storytellers, lived in the world of his imagination. But over time, as his fame grew, so did his pride. He began to care less for the inventions of his imagination than for the money his tales earned him. He became vain and often bragged that no other storyteller in the world could outdo him. Instead of wearing the rags of the poet and dreamer, he wore the rich robes of a prince. He even bought a fine Turkmen rug to decorate his house. True, it was small, but it was no ordinary rug. People thought Kasim ridiculous, but they still lined up to hear his stories.

One day, two young merchants from a village near the Aral Sea decided to play a trick on Kasim. They came up behind him where he was haggling with a fruit seller over an orange. Pretending not to notice him, they staged an argument.

"Kasim is the greatest storyteller alive!" said one.

Standardized Test Tutor: Reading (Grade 5) © 2009 by Michael Priestley, Scholastic Teaching Resources

"Not so," said the other. "Ali-djan from our village is better. He can make up taller tales."

Mortified, Kasim crept away. For days, he brooded over this insult. Then he decided to find this Ali-djan and challenge him to a contest over who could tell the taller tale.

After weeks of travel, Kasim came to the Aral Sea and the village of Ali-djan. As he knocked on the door of Ali-djan's house, he thought, "What a miserable little shack. Surely this man is not much of a storyteller!"

A little girl, about 6 years old, opened the door. She looked up at Kasim with eyes as black as the night, and told him that her father was not at home.

Kasim puffed himself up. "When he returns, tell your father that I, Kasim, have come all the way from Tashkent. I have brought him a Turkmen rug so long that one end is back in Tashkent and the other is on the ship that brought me here. I would like him to look at the end that is on the ship to see if he can use the rug in your small house."

"Ha!" thought Kasim to himself. "Let us see this Ali-djan try to outdo that tall tale!"

"Thank you," said the little girl. "This is perfect! You see, we have a Turkmen rug in our house. Yesterday a spark fell from the stove and burned a hole in our rug. Your rug sounds just the right size to patch that little hole!"

Kasim was shocked. If the 6-year-old daughter could outdo his tale this way, what would the father do? Without another word, he hurried back to his ship and rushed back home. He never bragged again.

Questions 1–5: Choose the best answer to each question.

1. Which element of the passage shows that it is a folktale?

Ⓐ The hero is a storyteller.

Ⓑ The passage begins with "Once there was . . ."

Ⓒ The setting is a city visited by many travelers.

Ⓓ The plot involves a complicated joke.

2. What is the main problem in this story?

Ⓐ Kasim irritates people because he is so vain.

Ⓑ Kasim earns too little money as a storyteller.

Ⓒ Kasim forgets how to tell interesting stories.

Ⓓ Kasim becomes less famous than Ali-djan.

3. The passage says, "*Mortified*, Kasim crept away." What is the meaning of *mortified*?

Ⓐ forgetful

Ⓑ embarrassed

Ⓒ delighted

Ⓓ suspicious

4. Why does Ali-djan's daughter tell Kasim the story about her family's Turkmen rug?

Ⓐ She is afraid of Kasim and wants him to think her family is rich.

Ⓑ She is sorry for her father and wants Kasim to help him.

Ⓒ She realizes what Kasim is doing and wants to tease him.

Ⓓ She is so young that she imitates whatever adults say.

5. What can you tell about Turkmen rugs from this story?

Ⓐ They are very valuable.

Ⓑ They are very large.

Ⓒ They come from Tashkent.

Ⓓ They are only for princes.

Standardized Test Tutor: Reading (Grade 5) © 2009 by Michael Priestley, Scholastic Teaching Resources

Directions: Read this passage about making butter. Then answer questions 6–11.

Make Your Own Butter

Did you know that you can make your own butter? It's quick, easy, fun, and delicious. Here's how:

1. Buy heavy or double cream from the grocery store.

2. Pour the cream into a food processor or an electric mixer. (You can also make butter by pouring it into a jar and shaking it by hand, but this takes a long time!)

3. Turn on the machine and beat it at a high speed for about seven minutes. (Make sure you use a deep bowl, or the cream will splatter all over the kitchen!)

4. After a few minutes, you will notice the cream start to thicken and form soft peaks. If you stopped here, you would have whipping cream. Mmm, tempting! But keep going; you're aiming for butter.

5. Eventually, you will see small flecks of yellow appear in the cream. You have made buttermilk. Buttermilk is good in all kinds of recipes, such as buttermilk pancakes. Keep going!

6. Suddenly, a lump of butter will separate from the buttermilk. Pour off the buttermilk and save it for those pancakes.

7. Wash the butter. I know it sounds odd, but if you don't rinse all of the buttermilk off your butter, the butter will turn sour.

8. To wash your butter, pour a little ice water on it.

9. Work the butter by pressing it with a fork to remove the water. Repeat this step several times.

10. If you like, you can flavor the butter. Many cooks like to add a pinch of salt. Others add more unusual flavorings, such as jam, lemon zest (peel), or herbs like rosemary or sage.

11. Finally, place your butter in a container or wrap it in wax paper, and enjoy! It will stay fresh in the refrigerator for approximately one week.

Questions 6–11: Choose the best answer to each question.

6. Which step is most important for making butter that tastes good?
   - Ⓐ using a food processor
   - Ⓑ adding salt
   - Ⓒ using a deep bowl
   - Ⓓ rinsing off the buttermilk

7. The author's main purpose in this passage is to—
   - Ⓐ encourage students to make their own foods.
   - Ⓑ compare store-bought butter and homemade butter.
   - Ⓒ explain a simple way to make butter from cream.
   - Ⓓ describe the science of how cream separates into butter and liquid.

8. According to the passage, you should remove water from the butter by—
   - Ⓐ squeezing by hand.
   - Ⓑ pressing with a fork.
   - Ⓒ using an electric mixer.
   - Ⓓ shaking it in a jar.

Standardized Test Tutor: Reading (Grade 5) © 2009 by Michael Priestley, Scholastic Teaching Resources

9. Most of the information in this passage is organized by—

   Ⓐ steps in a process.

   Ⓑ main idea and details.

   Ⓒ comparison/contrast.

   Ⓓ problem and solution.

10. What would happen if you stopped right after step 4?

   Ⓐ You would have buttermilk.

   Ⓑ You would have sour butter.

   Ⓒ You would have whipping cream.

   Ⓓ You would have thick butter.

11. What causes cream to turn into butter?

   Ⓐ refrigeration

   Ⓑ the addition of salt

   Ⓒ the addition of cold water

   Ⓓ rapid movement

Directions: Read this poem about getting ready for school.
Then answer questions 12–17.

Morning

I wake up to the radio, it's screeching in my ear.
Next door my sister's cell alarm wakes her.
The irritating buzzing from behind the bathroom door
Is my father's noisy electric razor.

My mother's in her bedroom, brandishing something.   5
The blow dryer howls around her wet dark hair.
She sees me in the hallway and moves her mouth a lot,
Saying something, but I just can't hear.

I tap my little brother's door; he's always last to rise.
There's no answer so I crack the door and peer.   10
He's up and dressed; he must have heard. Why didn't he answer me?
He smiles and points: an ear bud in each ear.

Down in the still-dark kitchen, a small beast begins to hiss.
It's the coffeemaker set to start at eight.
I pop bread in the toaster, pour some milk into a mug,   15
Then heat the milk up in the microwave.

Toast pops, milk dings, then comes a strange "blurb-blurbing" in the hall—
It's the automatic water for the cat.
The rumble from the basement means the furnace just switched on,
And the phone rings for a morning chat.   20

It's Nana. "Hi, Michelle, I'm glad I caught you before school.
Michelle, my dratted e-mail's on the blink!"
By the time I've talked her through the latest techni-woe,
My milk's cold so I pour it in the sink.

Now my dad's watching the morning news on his wide-screen TV,   25
While my mother listens to the radio.
My sister makes a smoothie out of frozen fruit and ice;
The blender grinds until I yell, "Hello!"

Am I the only one who's noticed that it's getting late?
I point to the clock on the stove without a word.   30
My sister gulps her smoothie, grabs her backpack and her coat,
We leave the house and stand out by the curb.

Outside the sun is shining and the birds sing in the trees,
"Nice day," my sister tells me with a smile.
She asks me how my science project's going, I say fine;   35
She says today she's going to run a mile.

She points to Mrs. Berry's yard; a crocus just popped up.
We say we can't wait till it's really spring.
We giggle when a neighbor and his little pup walk by.
The puppy holds its head up like a king.   40

We hear the bus from far away; we pick our backpacks up
From where we've had them lying on the ground.
The bus doors squeal open like a sighing animal;
There's something so alive about that sound!

My sister's friends call out to her, my friends call out to me.   45
We practice spelling words and check our math.
The school bus lets us off at school as the first bell rings.
We stop talking and hurry up the path.

—Stacey Sparks

Questions 12–17: Choose the best answer to each question.

12. Which word best describes the speaker in the poem?

Ⓐ responsible

Ⓑ shy

Ⓒ lazy

Ⓓ grumpy

13. In each stanza, which lines rhyme?

Ⓐ the first and second

Ⓑ the first and third

Ⓒ the second and fourth

Ⓓ the second and third

14. What happens just before Michelle leaves the house?

   Ⓐ Nana calls for help with her e-mail.

   Ⓑ Her mother dries her hair.

   Ⓒ The coffeemaker starts up.

   Ⓓ A neighbor and his puppy walk by.

15. How do the sisters act differently when they get outside the house?

   Ⓐ They worry about school.

   Ⓑ They depend on adults to tell them what to do.

   Ⓒ They help each other with their homework.

   Ⓓ They talk to each other.

16. What is the meaning of *brandishing* in line 5?

   Ⓐ fixing

   Ⓑ waving

   Ⓒ saying

   Ⓓ hiding

17. Which sentence expresses a theme of this poem?

   Ⓐ Modern technology runs people's lives.

   Ⓑ Children need more freedom to make decisions.

   Ⓒ Family members need to support one another.

   Ⓓ School is a child's most important responsibility.

Directions: Read this passage about a man named Carl Linnaeus. Then answer questions 18–24.

Carl Linnaeus

One of the world's greatest naturalists was born in Sweden 300 years ago. His name was Carl Linnaeus. Carl's father, a minister, loved flowers. He used them to decorate his son's cradle. Sometimes he gave flowers to young Carl to play with. Carl wanted to know the name of every plant he saw. Back then, the names of plants consisted of many Latin words strung together. The names were difficult for Carl to learn. Still, he was determined to memorize them.

Carl Linnaeus went away to school when he was 9. His parents planned for him to be a minister, like his father. Ministers needed to know Latin and Greek, so those were the subjects Carl had to study. But he found them boring. Sometimes he skipped class to search for flowers.

By the time Linnaeus reached high school, his teachers had decided that he would never become a minister. Luckily, a local doctor was impressed by Linnaeus's knowledge of plants. He thought that Carl should go to medical school. Back then, doctors needed to know about plants because they were used to make medicines.

At the university, Linnaeus continued to collect plants— hundreds of them! He decided that the way plants were grouped and named did not make sense. He began to make up a whole new system for organizing and naming every plant in the world.

One Christmas vacation, Linnaeus decided to take a trip to Lapland, a remote part of Scandinavia. The purpose was to study plants that did not grow in the south. Linnaeus also observed the local people. The Lapps were nomads who followed their herds of reindeer. Linnaeus was fascinated by how healthy the Lapps were. He decided that they were healthy because of their lifestyle. They got lots of exercise, breathed fresh air, got along well with one another, and did not overeat. Today many scientists think that exercise, a clean environment, happy relationships, and a good diet can help people stay healthy. Back in Linnaeus's day, these were new ideas. Much later in his life, Linnaeus gave public talks about these healthy habits.

Eventually, Linnaeus got his medical degree. His final essay was on the cause of malaria. He did not figure out that the disease was

Standardized Test Tutor: Reading (Grade 5) © 2009 by Michael Priestley, Scholastic Teaching Resources

transmitted by mosquitoes. (This discovery did not happen until around 1900.) But he noticed something important. Many people with malaria lived in houses built with clay. The clay was usually dug from a hole right next to the house, and the hole then filled with water. Mosquitoes breed in water.

Once, his curiosity almost got Linnaeus into trouble. He led a group of helpers to some islands off the coast of Sweden. They were looking for plants that could be used to make dyes and medicines. The local people got suspicious. They thought the scientists were spies from Sweden's enemy, Russia!

Linnaeus wrote a book about his island journey. He wrote the book in Swedish instead of in Latin, unlike most scientists. In it, he used his new system for naming plants. He gave each plant a two-part name. The names were still in Latin, but they were much easier to remember. They also made more sense. The first part of each name tells the group the plant belongs to. The second part describes something that makes the specific plant unique. Today, this two-part system is still used to name both plants and animals. He named one flower *Ranunculus acris*. *Ranunculus* refers to a genus (group) of similar flowers, and *acris* refers to the yellow flower in this group.

Despite his many achievements, Linnaeus was humble. He named only one flower after himself.

Questions 18–24: Choose the best answer to each question.

18. Linnaeus was one of the world's greatest *naturalists*. What does the word *naturalist* mean?

Ⓐ one who studies nature   Ⓒ against nature

Ⓑ of or related to nature   Ⓓ without nature

19. Which detail from the passage supports the idea that Linnaeus was very curious?

Ⓐ As a child, he sometimes played with flowers.

Ⓑ The names of flowers were hard for him to learn.

Ⓒ His teachers decided he would never be a minister.

Ⓓ One Christmas vacation, he decided to travel to Lapland.

Standardized Test Tutor: Reading (Grade 5) © 2009 by Michael Priestley, Scholastic Teaching Resources

20. In the author's view, what was Carl Linnaeus's most important contribution to science?

    Ⓐ observing what made the Lapps healthy

    Ⓑ creating a new system for naming plants

    Ⓒ finding new plant-based dyes and medicines

    Ⓓ discovering a cure for malaria

21. How were Linnaeus's plant names different from the older names?

    Ⓐ They were in Swedish.

    Ⓑ They were all named after people.

    Ⓒ They were shorter and simpler.

    Ⓓ They were named after medicines.

22. What did Linnaeus do just before he graduated from medical school?

    Ⓐ He wrote a book about a journey.

    Ⓑ He gave speeches about how to be healthy.

    Ⓒ He studied the causes of malaria.

    Ⓓ He started to collect flowers.

23. In Linnaeus's naming system, the second part of a plant's name refers to—

    Ⓐ its color.

    Ⓑ something that makes it unique.

    Ⓒ the family it belongs to.

    Ⓓ the number of petals it has.

24. What can you conclude about Carl Linnaeus?

    Ⓐ He was a careful observer.

    Ⓑ He was a lazy child.

    Ⓒ He was suspicious of others.

    Ⓓ He was an excellent doctor.

Directions: Read this passage about a strange camera.
Then answer questions 25–32.

The Camera

Manny got off the school bus and crossed the street. He was
starving! He opened his backpack, took out the key, and looked
forward to a snack. Then he noticed something on the porch that
had not been there this morning. Sitting on top of the container of
old newspapers was a tiny camera.

Manny knew the camera was not his mother's. She was a
photojournalist. Her camera was a professional model, and she
always kept it in a big canvas bag with her extra lenses. His mother
would laugh at a dinky little thing like this. Wondering, Manny
picked up the camera and went inside.

On the rug in the corner of the kitchen sat the kitten and the
dog. The kitten, which was a fraction of the dog's size, was licking
the dog's ears. So cute, thought Manny. He raised the mysterious
camera, turned it on, and clicked a picture. Then he looked at the
screen to check the image.

Something was wrong. The picture was crisp and clear, but Sylvie
was the wrong size. In the picture, she was no longer a tiny kitten but
a full-grown cat. Impossible!

Manny went outside and pointed the camera at the forsythia
bush. It was a cold spring, and the bush had not bloomed. Click!
Manny checked the photo. In it, the forsythia was a fountain of bright
yellow blossoms. Manny shivered.

Some kids would not have believed their eyes, but Manny
realized that this camera showed the future. He thought of all the
movies and comic books where the main character had the gift
of seeing the future. He always got mad because those characters
never used the gift in any good way!

Then Manny got an idea. His mother's morning paper lay folded
on the kitchen table with the front-page headline facing up. **CITY
HALL BURNS DOWN**! Manny thought for a minute. If he had found
the camera yesterday, maybe he could somehow have prevented
the fire! It was too late to prevent that disaster, but—Manny pointed
the mysterious camera at the front page and took a picture.

He checked the result. The print was hard to read on the
small screen, but the headline stood out. **WATER STREET
BRIDGE COLLAPSES**! Manny gasped. He strained to read the
rest of the story.

The bridge was going to collapse at 4:38 P.M. today. The cause would be a ship running into one of the giant columns that supported the bridge. The ship was named *The Dupree*, and it would be carrying iron ore. Something would go wrong with the steering.

With his heart pounding a hundred miles an hour, Manny picked up the phone and dialed information. He asked for the mayor's office.

When the mayor's assistant picked up, Manny said, "I would like to give an anonymous tip. I work on board a ship called *The Dupree*. We're scheduled to go through your town in about an hour, but conditions on board aren't safe. I can't say anything more, but you need to stop the boat *immediately* and have it inspected!"

The assistant said she would inform the mayor right away.

Manny stared at the camera in his shaking hand. He was too young for this responsibility! Suddenly, a message appeared on the screen.

"You did it!" it said, and then the screen went dead. Manny tried to turn the camera back on, but it was broken. He put it down and waited for the five o'clock news.

Questions 25–32: Choose the best answer to each question.

25. Manny tells the mayor's assistant that the boat needs to be *inspected*. The word *inspected* most likely means—

   Ⓐ "looked at closely."

   Ⓑ "stopped immediately."

   Ⓒ "turned aside."

   Ⓓ "cleaned thoroughly."

26. Manny's reaction when he sees the image of the forsythia covered with flowers shows that he is—

   Ⓐ dreamy.

   Ⓑ angry.

   Ⓒ cold.

   Ⓓ smart.

27. Manny first realizes that the camera can do something strange when he—

    (A) sees the camera on the porch.

    (B) sees the picture of the cat.

    (C) photographs the forsythia bush.

    (D) reads the headline about the bridge.

28. What is the most likely reason Manny gives the mayor's assistant a false explanation of how he knows the boat is in trouble?

    (A) He wants the assistant to believe him.

    (B) He does not want to get into trouble.

    (C) He thinks someone is watching him.

    (D) He enjoys making up stories.

29. The fact that Manny's heart was "pounding a hundred miles an hour" means that he was—

    (A) running to the phone.

    (B) hitting something.

    (C) beginning to get sick.

    (D) feeling very frightened.

30. The author describes the forsythia as "a fountain of bright yellow blossoms." This means that—

    (A) it is covered with many flowers.

    (B) its flowers are soaked by a spring rain.

    (C) its blossoms have fallen into a fountain.

    (D) it is just about to start blooming.

Standardized Test Tutor: Reading (Grade 5) © 2009 by Michael Priestley, Scholastic Teaching Resources

31. The author most likely wrote this passage to—

Ⓐ explain how accidents happen.

Ⓑ give information about cameras.

Ⓒ persuade readers to be careful.

Ⓓ tell an entertaining story.

32. Which sentence is the best summary of what happens in this story?

Ⓐ A boy dreams of being like the hero in a comic book.

Ⓑ A boy learns that a bridge is going to collapse.

Ⓒ A boy prevents a disaster by using a magic camera.

Ⓓ A boy finds a mysterious camera on his front porch.

Directions: Read these two passages about China.
Then answer questions 33–40.

Passage 1:
Snowstorms Affect New Year's Festivities

In late January and early February of 2008, a long series of freak snowstorms hit southern China and stopped all travel across the region. The impact was great because millions of Chinese were trying to get home for the New Year. Approximately 200,000 people were stranded at a single railway station. More than a dozen airports were closed.

Chinese New Year

The New Year is the most important holiday in China. The Chinese New Year falls between late January and late February. The festivities last for two weeks. They begin on the darkest day of the month (the day of the new moon) and end on the day of the full moon.

New Year's Traditions

Many traditions are associated with the New Year. Each year is named after a specific animal, such as the dragon, the boar, or the tiger. Children born in a certain year are supposed to have the characteristics of the animal for their year.

Red is the color of the New Year's celebrations because, in China, red stands for good luck. People wear red clothes. They decorate their homes with red. Children receive money in red envelopes.

The height of the festivities is the lantern festival. It falls on the 15th day of the first lunar month. People carry lanterns in a parade. Many of the lanterns are painted with beautiful designs.

New Year's Travel

Families gather to celebrate the New Year together. China has a population of more than 1 billion. During the holiday season, millions of people travel. But in 2008, the Year of the Rat, many travelers got stuck.

Standardized Test Tutor: Reading (Grade 5) © 2009 by Michael Priestley, Scholastic Teaching Resources

The government had to set up shelters in schools and other large spaces. Police stood by to keep order. Relief workers passed out quilts to keep families warm. Weather forecasters warned the Chinese to cancel their travel plans.

Many of those affected were workers who had migrated to large cities for manufacturing jobs. One such worker was Liu Si. Mr. Liu waited for days in the train station for a train to Chongqing before giving up. He had been living in Guangdong province for ten years. He said this was the first time he hadn't made it home for the New Year.

Other Storm-Related Problems

In some ways, the stranded travelers were lucky. At least they had safe places to stay. Elsewhere in China, more than 350,000 houses were destroyed by the bad weather. Electric lines were down, cutting off power. Water supplies and farmlands were damaged.

The End of the Storms

Luckily, as the New Year came to an end, so did the storms. The weather warmed. Red Cross staff members were able to deliver supplies to victims, and the government began working to repair the damage.

Passage 2:
Making a Chinese Lantern

A fun way to celebrate the Chinese New Year is to decorate your house with paper lanterns. They are easy decorations to make for this most important holiday.

Supplies

Colored construction paper	Pencil
Ruler	Yarn or ribbon
Tape or glue	Scissors
Decorations such as stickers and glitter (optional)	

Steps

1. Fold a piece of construction paper in half.

2. Place your ruler along the length of the paper, about 1 inch away from the edge opposite the folded edge, and draw a line. This will be the line where you will stop cutting.

3. Now place your ruler along the folded edge. Make a mark every inch.

4. Make a series of cuts from the folded edge up to the "stop" line.

5. Unfold the paper. Tape the edges of the paper together to make a lantern.

6. Cut another strip of paper about 6 inches long. Glue or tape the strip to the top of the lantern to make a handle.

7. If you wish, add stickers or glue glitter to your lantern. Then string yarn or ribbon through the handle and hang up your lantern!

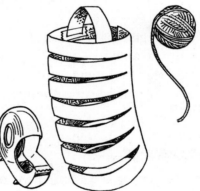

Standardized Test Tutor: Reading (Grade 5) © 2009 by Michael Priestley, Scholastic Teaching Resources

Questions 33–40: Choose the best answer to each question.

33. The passage says, "Approximately 200,000 people were *stranded* at a single railway station." Which definition of *strand* is used in this sentence?

> **strand** *verb* **1.** to drive onto shore; run aground.
> **2.** to leave in a helpless position. *noun* **3.** a fiber
> or thread twisted together to form a string or rope.
> **4.** the land bordering a body of water; beach.

Ⓐ definition 1

Ⓑ definition 2

Ⓒ definition 3

Ⓓ definition 4

34. Under which heading in Passage 1 is the lantern festival described?

Ⓐ **Chinese New Year**

Ⓑ **New Year's Traditions**

Ⓒ **New Year's Travel**

Ⓓ **Other Storm-Related Problems**

35. Under which heading in Passage 1 is the story of Mr. Liu told?

Ⓐ **Chinese New Year**

Ⓑ **New Year's Traditions**

Ⓒ **New Year's Travel**

Ⓓ **Other Storm-Related Problems**

36. The craft activity described in Passage 2 is most similar to—

Ⓐ making a bowl out of clay.

Ⓑ making a basket with strips of paper.

Ⓒ carving a jack-o'-lantern out of a pumpkin.

Ⓓ decorating an egg with crayons and dye.

37. Which detail best supports the statement that the Chinese New Year is the most important holiday in China?

Ⓐ Children born in a year are supposed to have the qualities of that year's animal.

Ⓑ The festivities begin on the darkest day of the first month and end on the day of the full moon.

Ⓒ Red is the color of the New Year's celebrations because red stands for good luck.

Ⓓ During the holiday season, millions of people travel.

38. Which sentence from Passage 2 is an opinion?

Ⓐ A fun way to celebrate the Chinese New Year is to decorate your house with paper lanterns.

Ⓑ This will be the line where you will stop cutting.

Ⓒ Tape the edges of the paper together to make a lantern.

Ⓓ If you wish, add stickers or glue glitter to your lantern.

39. What is the effect of taping the edges together in step 5 of Passage 2?

Ⓐ The lantern gets longer.

Ⓑ The lantern becomes circular.

Ⓒ The lantern gets a handle.

Ⓓ The lantern is hung up.

40. Both of these passages emphasize the idea that—

Ⓐ Chinese lanterns are fun and easy to make.

Ⓑ a series of snowstorms brought holiday travel to a halt.

Ⓒ the Chinese New Year is an important holiday.

Ⓓ more than a billion people live and travel in China.

End of Test 3 **STOP**

Standardized Test Tutor: Reading (Grade 5) © 2009 by Michael Priestley, Scholastic Teaching Resources

Standardized Test Tutor: Reading

Answer Sheet

Grade

Student Name _____

Teacher Name _____

Test 1 2 3
(circle one)

Directions: Fill in the bubble for the answer you choose.

1. Ⓐ Ⓑ Ⓒ Ⓓ   15. Ⓐ Ⓑ Ⓒ Ⓓ   29. Ⓐ Ⓑ Ⓒ Ⓓ

2. Ⓐ Ⓑ Ⓒ Ⓓ   16. Ⓐ Ⓑ Ⓒ Ⓓ   30. Ⓐ Ⓑ Ⓒ Ⓓ

3. Ⓐ Ⓑ Ⓒ Ⓓ   17. Ⓐ Ⓑ Ⓒ Ⓓ   31. Ⓐ Ⓑ Ⓒ Ⓓ

4. Ⓐ Ⓑ Ⓒ Ⓓ   18. Ⓐ Ⓑ Ⓒ Ⓓ   32. Ⓐ Ⓑ Ⓒ Ⓓ

5. Ⓐ Ⓑ Ⓒ Ⓓ   19. Ⓐ Ⓑ Ⓒ Ⓓ   33. Ⓐ Ⓑ Ⓒ Ⓓ

6. Ⓐ Ⓑ Ⓒ Ⓓ   20. Ⓐ Ⓑ Ⓒ Ⓓ   34. Ⓐ Ⓑ Ⓒ Ⓓ

7. Ⓐ Ⓑ Ⓒ Ⓓ   21. Ⓐ Ⓑ Ⓒ Ⓓ   35. Ⓐ Ⓑ Ⓒ Ⓓ

8. Ⓐ Ⓑ Ⓒ Ⓓ   22. Ⓐ Ⓑ Ⓒ Ⓓ   36. Ⓐ Ⓑ Ⓒ Ⓓ

9. Ⓐ Ⓑ Ⓒ Ⓓ   23. Ⓐ Ⓑ Ⓒ Ⓓ   37. Ⓐ Ⓑ Ⓒ Ⓓ

10. Ⓐ Ⓑ Ⓒ Ⓓ   24. Ⓐ Ⓑ Ⓒ Ⓓ   38. Ⓐ Ⓑ Ⓒ Ⓓ

11. Ⓐ Ⓑ Ⓒ Ⓓ   25. Ⓐ Ⓑ Ⓒ Ⓓ   39. Ⓐ Ⓑ Ⓒ Ⓓ

12. Ⓐ Ⓑ Ⓒ Ⓓ   26. Ⓐ Ⓑ Ⓒ Ⓓ   40. Ⓐ Ⓑ Ⓒ Ⓓ

13. Ⓐ Ⓑ Ⓒ Ⓓ   27. Ⓐ Ⓑ Ⓒ Ⓓ

14. Ⓐ Ⓑ Ⓒ Ⓓ   28. Ⓐ Ⓑ Ⓒ Ⓓ

Standardized Test Tutor: Reading (Grade 5) © 2009 by Michael Priestley, Scholastic Teaching Resources

Standardized Test Tutor: Reading (Grade 5) **73**

Test **1** Answer Key

1. D	**9.** C	**17.** C	**25.** C	**33.** D
2. A	**10.** B	**18.** D	**26.** C	**34.** C
3. D	**11.** A	**19.** C	**27.** B	**35.** A
4. B	**12.** D	**20.** D	**28.** D	**36.** B
5. D	**13.** C	**21.** A	**29.** C	**37.** B
6. B	**14.** B	**22.** C	**30.** A	**38.** D
7. A	**15.** A	**23.** B	**31.** C	**39.** A
8. D	**16.** A	**24.** C	**32.** B	**40.** D

Answer Key Explanations

The Card Maker

1. Correct response: **D**
(*Make predictions*)
   As Edwin gets out his art supplies, he realizes that the three empty spaces in the box of chocolates are thumb-size. Since he originally planned to make Grandma a tiny card, he will probably make three such cards and put them in the empty spaces.

Incorrect choices:

A Edwin feels guilty about eating three of the chocolates so he is more likely to give Grandma three little cards and the remaining chocolates.

B Edwin plans to make cards, not write an apology.

C He has taken out his art supplies, not baking ingredients.

2. Correct response: **A**
(*Analyze characters*)
   Edwin is greedy because he eats some of the chocolates, but he is also kindhearted because he wants to do something special for his grandmother.

2. (continued)
Incorrect choices:

B Edwin does seem creative, but he is not lazy; he works hard on his projects.

C Edwin may be honest, but he and his ideas are not dull.

D Edwin is determined to make something for his grandmother but is not sad about it.

3. Correct response: **D**
(*Identify literary devices*)
   A simile compares two things and uses the word *like* or *as*.

Incorrect choices:

A This sentence does not use hyperbole, or exaggeration.

B A metaphor does not use the word *like* or *as*.

C This sentence does not make an object seem to act like a person.

4. Correct response: **B**
(*Identify cause and effect*)
   Edwin ate the cherry chocolate to fill the hollow feeling in his stomach—a sign that he was upset.

4. (continued)

Incorrect choices:

A He did not know it was a cherry chocolate until he ate it.

C The passage says that Grandma hates coconut, not cherry chocolate.

D He opened the box at first to see if the chocolates were "nice and fresh," but that is not why he ate the cherry chocolate.

5. Correct response: **D**
(*Evaluate author's purpose*)
   This is an entertaining story about a boy who eats some of the chocolates he bought for his grandmother.

Incorrect choices:

A This passage does not explain how to make a birthday card.

B This is not a persuasive passage written to remind people of something.

C This passage does not teach a lesson about respecting older people.

Hatching Eggs Without a Hen

6. Correct response: **B**
(*Identify synonyms*)
   Mechanism and *device* have almost the same meaning, so they are synonyms.

Incorrect choices:

A *Incubate* and *borrow* have very different meanings; they are not synonyms.

C The *coating* on the outside of an egg and the *contents* (on the inside) are not the same.

D *Germ* and *disease* are related to each other but do not mean the same thing.

7. Correct response: **A**
(*Make inferences*)
   The instructions say that washing an egg removes its protective coating and allows disease to pass through the shell.

7. (continued)

Incorrect choices:

B Eggs can be turned by hand or machine

C Eggs bought over the Internet are probably sent through the mail.

D The table indicates that eggs should not be turned just before they hatch.

8. Correct response: **D**
(*Interpret graphic features: table*)
   According to the table, goose eggs take the longest (28–34 days) to hatch.

Incorrect choices:

A Chicken eggs take 21 days.

B Turkey eggs take 28 days.

C Duck eggs take 28 days.

9. Correct response: **C**
(*Identify sequence of events*)
   According to the last paragraph, the first thing a chick does after breaking out of its shell is to clean its feathers.

Incorrect choices:

A The chick drinks water after it cleans its feathers.

B The chick eats after it cleans its feathers.

D A baby bird cannot lay an egg just after it hatches.

10. Correct response: **B**
(*Use prefixes and suffixes to determine word meaning*)
   The prefix *dis-* means "not," and *-ant* is a noun suffix, so *disinfectant* refers to something that does not allow infection.

Incorrect choices:

A The suffix *-ant* usually refers to a thing, not a person.

C The prefix *dis-* indicates that germs would not grow.

D The word *disinfectant* is a noun, not an adjective.

11. Correct response: **A**
(*Draw conclusions*)
   The emphasis on selecting an egg based on its appearance suggests that cracked, dirty, oddly shaped, undersize, or oversize eggs are likely to have problems.

Incorrect choices:

B The passage gives no evidence to support this conclusion.

C The passage suggests that all of the birds listed in the table hatch in the same way.

D The passage says that the chicks use their beaks for cleaning.

Ronald the Painter

12. Correct response: **D**
(*Use context clues to determine word meaning*)
   The door is covered with spots of different colors, and the family analyzes each hue.

Incorrect choices:

A The family has to choose a color, not a kind of paint.

B Ronald has offered several different colors, not different ideas.

C The "cool door" is Ronald's gift to the family, but that is not a hue.

13. Correct response: **C**
(*Interpret poetry and its characteristics*)
   In every stanza, the second and fourth lines rhyme. Sometimes the first and third lines rhyme as well.

Incorrect choices:

A The story takes place in one setting, at the family's home.

B The poem uses two similes in the first stanza, but those are the only comparisons.

D There are no talking animal characters in the poem.

14. Correct response: **B**
(*Compare and contrast*)
   In lines 1 to 24, Joseph (the speaker) seems annoyed at Ron's loudness, his constant comments, and his silly jokes. By the end, Joseph appreciates Ron's good-natured friendliness and realizes that the family will miss him.

Incorrect choices:

A There is no evidence that Joseph distrusts Ron.

C Joseph might admire Ron at the end but does not feel this way in the beginning.

D Joseph cannot seem to avoid Ron, so he certainly notices him.

15. Correct response: **A**
(*Analyze characters*)
   Ron is outgoing and friendly to everyone.

Incorrect choices:

B Ron talks to and interrupts everyone, so he is not shy.

C Ron works hard to finish the job, so he is not lazy.

D Ron makes comments to everyone whether they like it or not, so he is not very polite.

16. Correct response: **A**
(*Analyze literary elements: plot*)
   Line 44 says that there was "wind, rain, and hail" on Thursday.

Incorrect choices:

B The family creeps out the back on Saturday.

C Rebecca tells Ron a joke on Wednesday.

D The family chooses blue on Saturday.

17. Correct response: **C**
(*Identify cause and effect*)
   Lines 46 to 48 explain that Ron is "quiet and sad" because he did not complete the job before the big storm, as he had promised.

17. (continued)
   Incorrect choices:

   A Ron is quiet for the first time, but not because he realizes he has been too noisy.

   B Ron tells the family that midnight blue is an "awesome choice."

   D There's no indication that Ron will miss the family.

Police Arrest Unruly Neighbors

18. Correct response: **D**
   (*Use context clues to determine word meaning*)
   Blasting music and heaving ornaments into the neighbor's yard are ways of fighting back.

   Incorrect choices:

   A Mr. Levesque opened the windows to fight back, not because he was backing down.

   B Mr. Levesque did not complain by opening the windows; he fought back.

   C Mr. Levesque wanted triumph over his neighbor, not sympathy.

19. Correct response: **C**
   (*Identify main idea and details*)
   Ryan Southpaw and Jerome Levesque are former friends who get involved in a series of disputes after Southpaw criticizes Levesque's bumper sticker.

   Incorrect choices:

   A These neighbors use their lawns for protests; they are not competing for the best landscaping.

   B They may have differing tastes in music, but this is not the cause of the dispute.

   D This sentence gives a detail from the passage, not the main idea.

20. Correct response: **D**
   (*Distinguish fact and opinion*)
   This sentence gives a personal feeling or view that cannot be verified as fact.

20. (continued)
   Incorrect choices:

   A and **C** are factual statements that can be proven true.

   B is a generalization that does not express an opinion.

21. Correct response: **A**
   (*Identify cause and effect*)
   Paragraphs 6 to 8 explain what first made Mr. Southpaw upset a year ago.

   Incorrect choices:

   B Mr. Levesque played heavy metal music this year to irritate his neighbor, but this was not the cause of the problem.

   C This was a result of the ongoing dispute, but not the original problem.

   D This may have been true, but it was not the cause of the original problem.

22. Correct response: **C**
   (*Evaluate author's point of view*)
   Comments such as "The ammunition was opera" (paragraph 3) and "an anti-concrete-bunny rule" (paragraph 15) suggest that the reporter is amused.

   Incorrect choices:

   A, **B**, and **D** are incorrect. There is no indication that the reporter is horrified by these events, saddened by them, or furious at the situation.

23. Correct response: **B**
   (*Interpret figurative language, including idioms*)
   This is an idiom that means becoming upset.

   Incorrect choices:

   A This idiom does not refer to planning or causing destruction.

   C This is a literal interpretation of the phrase.

   D This is a plausible guess but is not the meaning of the idiom.

24. Correct response: **C**
(*Use details or evidence from the text to support ideas*)

There are no laws against having painted ornaments on your lawn, so the police cannot help Mr. Southpaw when he complains about Mr. Levesque's ornaments.

Incorrect choices:

A Mr. Levesque bought the concrete bunnies from Ollie's as or because it was going out of business; it does not affect the police.

B and **D** Ryan Southpaw's actions were not relevant to the fact that the police could do nothing.

The Birth of the Green World

25. Correct response: **C**
(*Analyze literary elements: plot*)

The gods cover all of the plants so that Mira will not hurt her foot again, but the humans need plants to survive.

Incorrect choices:

A There isn't any food for the animals or the humans.

B Mira's father wants to protect her but does not want to keep her at home.

D The people are not fighting the gods, for the gods are clearly in control.

26. Correct response: **C**
(*Analyze literary elements: plot*)

The red-haired girl suggests grass as a solution: it is soft underfoot but is also a plant.

Incorrect choices:

A Mira liked the carpet and did not suggest any other solution.

B Hall liked the idea of grass but was not the one who suggested it.

D Graybeak is mentioned in the story but does not play a part beyond making it rain.

27. Correct response: **B**
(*Analyze literary elements: setting*)

The third paragraph says that Mira was walking in a valley near her home.

Incorrect choices:

A She lived on Mount Gorash but was walking in a valley.

C The Weavers of Dorn lived in a cave, but Mira was not there.

D She was near Mount Gorash but was not at home.

28. Correct response: **D**
(*Compare and contrast*)

The gods never grow sick or old, so they do not die.

Incorrect choices:

A Mira feels pain when she hurts her foot.

B They do eat, but their food is different from people's food.

C They do sleep; Hall got upset when the "racket" woke him up.

29. Correct response: **C**
(*Analyze characters*)

He likes the idea of covering Earth with something his daughter would enjoy even more than the carpet.

Incorrect choices:

A The carpet did not keep the people quiet, and neither will the grass.

B He doesn't show any concern for the animals.

D He is the greatest of gods and does not have to prove himself.

30. Correct response: **A**
(*Interpret figurative language, including idioms*)

The man is telling Fen that if the carpet remains on Earth, then nothing will grow and all living things will die.

30. (continued)
Incorrect choices:

B The carpet was gray, like smoke, but that is not what this sentence means.

C This sentence has nothing to do with setting a fire.

D This is a plausible idea but is not the meaning of the sentence.

31. Correct response: **C**
(*Identify literary genres and their characteristics*)
This story is a myth because it begins with the phrase "Long ago," it has gods as characters, and it attempts to explain a natural phenomenon (grass).

Incorrect choices:

A A biography tells the life story of a real person.

B Science fiction is generally set in the future and involves the use of science or technology.

D Realistic fiction tells about something that could happen in real life.

32. Correct response: **B**
(*Analyze literary elements: theme*)
Hall wants to solve the problem one way (with a carpet), but the little girl thinks of another way (grass).

Incorrect choices:

A This theme does not fit the story because it refers to a bad situation (a "cloud") that actually has a good side to it (the "silver lining").

C The people could not be patient because if they were, they would die.

D The people did not ignore the problem, and it did not get worse.

Bread and Oatmeal Bread

33. Correct response: **D**
(*Use context clues to determine word meaning*)
The explanation of leavening agents in paragraphs 5 and 6 follows the question of what makes the dough rise.

Incorrect choices:

A A leavening agent is not a type of bread; it is used in making bread.

B A mill or grinder turns grain into flour.

C Leavening agents produce gas or air bubbles, but they are not gases themselves.

34. Correct response: **C**
(*Use details or evidence from the text to support ideas*)
The fact that laws were passed hundreds of years ago to control bread prices and keep it affordable is strong evidence for how important it was.

Incorrect choices:

A The fact that Egyptian rulers had bread in their tombs does not prove how important it was for all kinds of people.

B Arguing over the taste of bread does not prove how important it was to everyone.

D The fact that some people brought their breads to a bake house does not show that bread was a very important food.

35. Correct response: **A**
(*Identify main idea and supporting details*)
The main idea of **The Magic Ingredient** is that yeast makes bread dough rise, and that gives bread its special texture.

Incorrect choices:

B The process may have seemed magical, but that is not the main idea of the section.

C This sentence gives a detail from the section but not the main idea.

D This is a detail from another section.

36. Correct response: **B**
(*Identify sequence of events*)

You must cook the oats (step 1) before adding molasses to them (step 3).

Incorrect choices:

A Adding yeast takes place in step 4, after adding the molasses.

C Adding flour takes place in step 5, after adding the molasses.

D Kneading the dough takes place in step 6, after adding the molasses.

37. Correct response: **B**
(*Summarize*)

This passage is a recipe that tells what ingredients you will need and how to make oatmeal bread.

Incorrect choices:

A This passage tells about only one kind of oatmeal bread.

C This information is given in the chart but is not the main topic of the passage.

D This information does not appear in the passage.

38. Correct response: **D**
(*Distinguish fact and opinion*)

This sentence expresses a personal view that cannot be proven true.

Incorrect choices:

A, **B**, and **C** all state facts that can be verified.

39. Correct response: **A**
(*Use graphic features: chart*)

The chart indicates that large holes are a result of bread rising too long.

Incorrect choices:

B This is the result of not cooking the bread long enough.

C This happens when the dough is not mixed enough.

D This happens when the loaf is not baked in the center of the oven.

40. Correct response: **D**
(*Make connections*)

A reader would have to know how to knead dough because neither passage explains how to do this.

Incorrect choices:

A Passage 1 explains how to proof yeast.

B Passage 2 explains how to cook oats.

C Passage 2 explains how to tell when a loaf of bread is finished.

Test **2** Answer Key

1. D	**9.** C	**17.** B	**25.** A	**33.** D
2. B	**10.** B	**18.** A	**26.** C	**34.** C
3. C	**11.** D	**19.** C	**27.** D	**35.** B
4. B	**12.** D	**20.** B	**28.** D	**36.** D
5. A	**13.** B	**21.** B	**29.** C	**37.** A
6. B	**14.** C	**22.** C	**30.** A	**38.** A
7. A	**15.** A	**23.** D	**31.** D	**39.** C
8. D	**16.** D	**24.** B	**32.** B	**40.** B

Answer Key Explanations

Fungi

1. Correct response: **D**
(*Use etymology, root words, and word origins to determine word meaning*)
The word *dormant* means "not active, or asleep." It has the same root as *dormitory*, which is a building where students sleep.

Incorrect choices:

A Being inactive is not like taking a trip.

B Becoming dormant does not involve eating.

C Being inactive does not include searching for shelter.

2. Correct response: **B**
(*Identify main idea and supporting details*)
Special Features begins with the question of what makes fungi different from plants and animals, and that is the main topic.

2. (continued)
Incorrect choices:

A What fungi look like is a topic in the first part of the passage.

C Uses of fungi are described in **Harmful or Beneficial?**

D When types of fungi were discovered is described under **Harmful or Beneficial?**

3. Correct response: **C**
(*Evaluate author's purpose*)
This passage is an informational article about fungi. Its purpose is to inform readers.

Incorrect choices:

A This passage does not help readers recognize types of fungi.

B This is not a narrative passage written to entertain.

D This passage does not compare mushrooms and other fungi.

4. Correct response: **B**
(*Distinguish fact and opinion*)
    This sentence expresses a personal view that cannot be verified as fact.

Incorrect choices:

A and **C** state facts that can be proven true.

D uses a metaphor to describe fungi, but it does not express an opinion.

5. Correct response: **A**
(*Draw conclusions*)
    Fungi do not need sunlight to survive because they do not have chlorophyll, which combines with sunlight to make food for plants.

Incorrect choices:

B Fungi can become dormant whether there is sunlight or not.

C Fungi depend on wind or some other outside force to move them, but this is not related to sunlight.

D The ability to float through the air is not related to sunlight.

The First Music

6. Correct response: **B**
(*Identify literary genres and their characteristics*)
    Myths often include gods, and they usually explain how something in nature came about.

Incorrect choices:

A Dialogue is used in many kinds of literature, not just myths.

C Presenting a solution to a problem may be a feature of many kinds of fiction, or even some kinds of nonfiction.

D A mysterious setting is not required for, or unique to, a myth.

7. Correct response: **A**
(*Interpret figurative language including idioms*)
    The next-to-last paragraph says, "The music rose to the surface of Earth like bubbles rising to the surface of a lake."

7. (continued)
Incorrect choices:

B The passage says that other sounds mixed with the sound of Earth's heartbeat.

C The crash of waves was one of the sounds that Ah Kin Xooc gathered.

D The patter of raindrops was one of the sounds Ah Kin Xooc gathered.

8. Correct response: **D**
(*Analyze literary elements: plot*)
    The gods realize that people lack music, which is a way to express their feelings.

Incorrect choices:

A A lack of appreciation was not the concern of the gods in the story.

B This was not the problem because Earth did have a living heart.

C There is no evidence in the story that the people wanted to be gods.

9. Correct response: **C**
(*Use context clues to determine word meaning*)
    The people's *melancholy* faces are contrasted with their strength and health, suggesting that they are sad despite all of the food and comforts they have been given.

Incorrect choices:

A The people move slowly and never sing, but they show no signs of anger.

B The passage says they are strong and healthy, so their faces are probably not thin.

D The gods had forgotten music, but the people were not forgetful.

10. Correct response: **B**
(*Identify sequence of events*)
    The next-to-last paragraph says that right after Ah Kin Xooc opened his mouth and let out the sounds, they mixed with Earth's heartbeat.

10. (continued)

Incorrect choices:

A The gods provided the sounds, so they had listened to them before.

C The sounds spread "far and wide," but that was after they mixed with the heartbeat.

D The people turned the sounds into songs after the sounds mixed with Earth's heartbeat.

11. Correct response: **D**
(*Analyze literary elements: theme*)
People have everything they need to meet their physical needs at the beginning of the story, but they are not happy until they have music.

Incorrect choices:

A, **B**, and **C** are incorrect. The passage does not support any of these themes.

Seeing the Moon

12. Correct response: **D**
(*Interpret figurative language*)
Describing the moon as "staring calmly" makes it seem like a person.

Incorrect choices:

A is an example of sight imagery, not personification.

B and **C** are examples of metaphor (calling a cloud a blanket and the moon a coin).

13. Correct response: **B**
(*Analyze literary elements: setting*)
You can tell from line 8 that they are in the kitchen.

Incorrect choices:

A They go outside their house later in the poem, but not outside a school.

C Using a telescope might suggest a science museum, but they are at home.

D They go outside later in the poem, but they are in the kitchen at the beginning.

14. Correct response: **C**
(*Compare and contrast*)
At first the father doesn't realize that his son has no interest in seeing the eclipse. At the end of the poem, the father understands his son's true feelings and sees him as a real person.

Incorrect choices:

A He still thinks that the eclipse is important.

B He seems glad that he brought his son outside, not sorry.

D They seem to get along well already, so he doesn't change in this way.

15. Correct response: **A**
(*Identify literary devices*)
The poet uses sight imagery throughout the poem ("seeing the moon," "a rusty sphere," "blotches of brown," and so on).

Incorrect choices:

B There are no real sounds in the poem, other than some dialogue.

C The poet mentions a "warm kitchen" and "something hot to drink," but she uses sight images much more than words related to heat.

D There is an unspoken love between the father and son, but this is not described in words or images.

16. Correct response: **D**
(*Interpret poetry and its characteristics*)
Alliteration is the use of repeated initial sounds, like the "b" sounds in "big blotches of brown."

Incorrect choices:

A, **B**, and **C** do not contain examples of alliteration.

17. Correct response: **B**
(*Interpret poetry and its characteristics*)
The speaker repeats the word *world* to show that he is suddenly aware of and amazed by the vastness of the universe.

17. (continued)

Incorrect choices:

A The speaker may feel impressed or awed, but he is not upset.

C This is an example of repetition, not rhyme.

D The speaker feels "dizzy" and amazed; there is no evidence that he feels tired at this point.

From the *Darnell Elementary School Eagle*

18. Correct response: **A**
(*Use reference aids to clarify meaning: dictionary*)
In this sentence, the word *propose* means "to suggest."

Incorrect choices:

B, **C**, and **D** are all meanings of *propose*, but none of them fits in this sentence.

19. Correct response: **C**
(*Identify text structure/organization*)
The writer tells how he thinks recess should be scheduled and then gives many reasons why this is a good plan.

Incorrect choices:

A, **B**, and **D** are different ways to organize text, but none of them describes this passage.

20. Correct response: **B**
(*Identify cause and effect*)
In point 3, the author argues that unstructured activity allows kids to make their own decisions about what they want to do.

Incorrect choices:

A The author says that taking a break and resting can help improve concentration.

C The author does not suggest that unstructured activity will lead to calmer, more polite kids.

D In point 4, the author says that more exercise will make kids stronger.

21. Correct response: **B**
(*Identify main idea and supporting details*)
The main idea of point 2 is that kids don't have the same opportunities to play freely with other kids as their parents did.

Incorrect choices:

A The author says that kids need to spend more time with other kids, not with their parents.

C This is a detail under point 2 but not the main idea.

D The author says that parents make their kids stay in, perhaps because they think the world is dangerous, but this is not the main idea.

22. Correct response: **C**
(*Use details or evidence from the text to support ideas*)
The writer says that he came up with his idea after doing "careful research on the Internet," and he has "found many scientific reasons to back my proposal."

Incorrect choices:

A He mentions couch potatoes in point 4 but gives no supporting evidence.

B He states that he is not lazy but does not offer "research" to prove it.

D Doing research on the Internet is not related to taking breaks from classes.

23. Correct response: **D**
(*Distinguish essential and nonessential information*)
This detail is least essential because it does not help the author's argument.

Incorrect choices:

A, **B**, and **C** are important details because they all help the author's argument.

24. Correct response: **B**
(*Summarize*)
This summary includes the author's proposal to make recess longer and the three major arguments in favor of it.

24. (continued)

Incorrect choices:

A This sentence gives background information but is not a summary of the passage.

C This is a detail from the passage but not a summary.

D This sentence gives a generalization based on parts of the passage but not a summary of the whole piece.

Summer Camp

25. Correct response: **A**
(*Use etymology, root words, and word origins to determine word meaning*)

The word *repellent* comes from *repel*, which means to "drive away." Mosquito repellent drives mosquitoes away, or keeps them off.

Incorrect choices:

B The *-ent* suffix usually indicates a thing, not a person.

C The parts of this word do not suggest anything that soothes the itch.

D Something that repels mosquitoes gets rid of them; it does not trap them.

26. Correct response: **C**
(*Identify cause and effect*)

The fourth paragraph says that Ketia would rather stay at home but does not want to disappoint her mother and her aunt.

Incorrect choices:

A She does not hear about the other kids until she is already there.

B She thinks staying at home would be fun, not boring.

D Ketia doesn't show any interest in North Carolina, where the camp is located.

27. Correct response: **D**
(*Analyze literary elements: setting*)

The setting is crucial to the story because it allows Ketia to have an interesting experience far from home and her friends.

27. (continued)

Incorrect choices:

A Ketia does not learn any important truths about her family, just the names of some of her aunt's old camping friends.

B The story does not suggest any conflicts in values.

C Ketia expects to have some problems, but everything goes smoothly.

28. Correct response: **D**
(*Analyze characters*)

As Ketia stumbles exhaustedly toward the car, her aunt frowns from worry because she can see that her niece is having trouble.

Incorrect choices:

A Aunt Marjorie sighs because Ketia asks her the same question more than once.

B Aunt Marjorie makes this offer because she wants Ketia to have the same kind of experience she had.

C Aunt Marjorie's waving shows her own excitement about the camp, not an awareness of others.

29. Correct response: **C**
(*Analyze literary elements: plot*)

When Ketia realizes that swimming in the lake is even more fun than swimming in the pool back home, her whole feeling about camp changes.

Incorrect choices:

A Ketia seems to enjoy being welcomed by name, but this is not a major turning point.

B Learning camp songs seems to be fun, but this is not a major turning point.

D Ketia's feelings about the camp changed before she tie-dyed a T-shirt.

30. Correct response: **A**
(*Analyze characters*)

Nellie is always positive and cheerful, saying "Awesome," and proclaiming that the camp is the best ever.

30. (continued)
Incorrect choices:

B Nellie seems quite relaxed, not strict.

C Nellie seems excitable and is always moving, so she is not really calm.

D Nellie plans a tie-dye activity, so she may be artistic, but this does not describe her as well as "cheerful."

31. Correct response: **D**
(*Make connections*)
Entering a new school would best help a reader understand Ketia's feelings because it would involve a new place, new friends and activities, and new rules.

Incorrect choices:

A There isn't anything competitive about going to the camp.

B The reader would probably know his or her cousins and would be in a familiar place.

C The reader would be in a familiar class with his or her friends.

32. Correct response: **B**
(*Make inferences, predictions, and generalizations*)
Ketia fears that she will get sore from hauling her backpack around, and she does.

Incorrect choices:

A Ketia expects to be lonely, but she is not.

C Ketia expects to be bored at camp, but she is not.

D She was worried about finding her group, but Nellie knew right away who she was.

Jane Goodall and Chimpanzees

33. Correct response: **D**
(*Identify main idea and supporting details*)
The main idea can be inferred from the first two paragraphs.

33. (continued)
Incorrect choices:

A This statement is a generalization, not the main idea.

B This sentence gives supporting details, not the main idea.

C This sentence gives a main idea from Passage 2.

34. Correct response: **C**
(*Identify main idea and supporting details*)
The fact that Goodall worked with Leakey looking for fossils in Africa shows her willingness to work hard.

Incorrect choices:

A This was one of her dreams but does not show that she worked hard.

B Taking a trip to Africa does not demonstrate a willingness to work.

D This detail describes one thing she liked about her job but does not show that she worked hard.

35. Correct response: **B**
(*Identify cause and effect*)
Jane learned from watching a hen when she was 5 that she had to be patient to observe animals.

Incorrect choices:

A She rode horses, but they did not teach her about observation.

C She learned a lot about animal nature, not patience, from the dog Rusty.

D As children, she and her friends raced snails, but they did not teach her about observation.

36. Correct response: **D**
(*Make inferences*)
Goodall left the Leakeys because she wanted to study living animals, not fossils.

36. (continued)

Incorrect choices:

A She chose to work in remote places and probably didn't feel lonely.

B She took advice from Dr. Leakey when he suggested studying chimpanzees.

C Being surrounded by wild animals was her favorite part of the job.

37. Correct response: **A**
(*Use text features*)

The headings are used to help the reader find information quickly and easily.

Incorrect choices:

B The headings are useful descriptions, not clever sayings.

C The headings indicate the subject of each section but do not sum up the information.

D The headings tell what each section is about but do not encourage questions.

38. Correct response: **A**
(*Summarize*)

This section explains that chimps can communicate vocally, through gestures and facial expressions, and, in some cases, through sign language.

Incorrect choices:

B, **C**, and **D** give details from the section but do not summarize the important information.

39. Correct response: **C**
(*Compare and contrast*)

Under **Chimpanzee Behavior**, the passage says that chimpanzees, like humans, live in groups, and some members of the group become more powerful than others.

Incorrect choices:

A There is no suggestion that only some chimpanzees use tools.

B All chimpanzees seem to live in large groups, not just some.

D Humans tend to stay with their mothers much longer than chimpanzees.

40. Correct response: **B**
(*Make connections*)

Both passages describe chimpanzees and how intelligent they are.

Incorrect choices:

A Jane Goodall is mentioned only in Passage 1.

C Only Passage 1 describes what Jane Goodall did.

D This information is mentioned only in Passage 2.

1. B	**9.** A	**17.** A	**25.** A	**33.** B
2. A	**10.** C	**18.** A	**26.** D	**34.** B
3. B	**11.** D	**19.** D	**27.** B	**35.** C
4. C	**12.** A	**20.** B	**28.** A	**36.** B
5. A	**13.** C	**21.** C	**29.** D	**37.** D
6. D	**14.** A	**22.** C	**30.** A	**38.** A
7. C	**15.** D	**23.** B	**31.** D	**39.** B
8. B	**16.** B	**24.** A	**32.** C	**40.** C

Answer Key Explanations

Kasim's Lesson

1. Correct response: **B**
(*Identify literary genres and their characteristics*)
The way this story begins is characteristic of a folktale.

Incorrect choices:

A This does not make the story a folktale; many other kinds of literature could include a storyteller.

C This kind of setting is not unique to folktales; it could be used in other kinds of stories.

D Any kind of fiction could include a complicated joke.

2. Correct response: **A**
(*Analyze literary elements: plot*)
The second paragraph explains that Kasim became vain and bragged that no other storyteller could outdo him.

2. (continued)
Incorrect choices:

B Kasim makes enough money to wear nice robes and buy an expensive rug.

C Kasim irritates people, but they still line up to hear his stories.

D Kasim still seems to be the most famous storyteller, but he realizes that others may be better than he.

3. Correct response: **B**
(*Use context clues to determine word meaning*)
Kasim thinks he is the best storyteller in the world, so he is deeply embarrassed when he hears that people think someone else is better.

Incorrect choices:

A *Forgetful* does not fit in the context of the sentence.

C Kasim could have been delighted, but the fact that he "crept away" and "brooded" suggests that he was embarrassed or worried.

D Kasim could have been suspicious, but this is not the meaning of *mortified*.

4. Correct response: **C**
(*Analyze characters*)
Ali-djan's daughter seems to be very clever, and she outdoes Kasim with little effort.

Incorrect choices:

A The girl does not seem frightened of Kasim at all.

B There is no indication of how the daughter feels about her father, and she does not ask Kasim for help.

D The response she gives is spontaneous and a perfect answer to Kasim's story, so she could not be imitating or copying someone else's response.

5. Correct response: **A**
(*Make inferences*)
The second paragraph suggests that Turkmen rugs are expensive and are not "ordinary," so they must be valuable.

Incorrect choices:

B The rug Kasim has is small, but he pretends his is very large.

C Kasim buys his rug in Tashkent, but it is a trade center for travelers from many places. Turkmen rugs come from the land of the Turkmens (now called Turkmenistan).

D Kasim has a Turkmen rug but is not a prince, even though he "wore the rich robes of a prince."

Make Your Own Butter

6. Correct response: **D**
(*Distinguish essential and nonessential information*)
Step 7 says that the butter will turn sour if you don't rinse off the buttermilk.

Incorrect choices:

A Using a food processor is not essential, since you can make butter in other ways.

B Step 10 says that many cooks like to add a little salt, but this is not essential.

C The size of the bowl would not affect the taste.

7. Correct response: **C**
(*Evaluate author's purpose*)
This passage is a recipe, or how-to article, explaining how to make butter.

Incorrect choices:

A This is not a persuasive passage meant to encourage students.

B The author does not compare store-bought and homemade butter.

D This passage indirectly describes the science but that is not its main purpose.

8. Correct response: **B**
(*Use text features*)
Step 9 says that you should work the butter with a fork to remove the water.

Incorrect choices:

A, **C**, and **D** are incorrect. These procedures may be used in other parts of the process, but they are not recommended for removing water.

9. Correct response: **A**
(*Identify text structure/organization*)
This passage is a recipe that describes steps in a process.

Incorrect choices:

B, **C**, and **D** are other ways to organize and present information, but they are not used as the main text structure in this passage.

10. Correct response: **C**
(*Identify sequence of events*)
After completing step 4, you would have whipping cream.

Incorrect choices:

A You would have buttermilk after step 5.

B You would have sour butter if you didn't complete step 7.

D You would have thick butter after step 6.

11. Correct response: **D**
(*Identify cause and effect*)
Cream turns into butter when it is mixed or beaten rapidly for a long time.

11. (continued)

Incorrect choices:

A Butter should be refrigerated after it is made, but this is not what causes cream to turn into butter.

B Salt can be added to the recipe, but this is not what makes butter.

C Cold water is used to wash off the buttermilk after the cream has turned into butter.

Morning

12. Correct response: **A**
(*Analyze characters*)
    The speaker gets up on time, makes breakfast, and gets her sister to the bus stop, so she is responsible.

Incorrect choices:

B The speaker meets her friends and does not seem shy.

C The speaker gets up on time, makes breakfast, and practices and does her homework, so she does not seem lazy.

D The speaker smiles and giggles and chats, so she doesn't seem grumpy.

13. Correct response: **C**
(*Interpret poetry and its characteristics*)
    The second and fourth lines rhyme in each stanza (as in *her* and *razor* in the first stanza).

Incorrect choices:

A, **B**, and **D** are incorrect. These pairs of lines do not rhyme in this poem.

14. Correct response: **A**
(*Identify sequence of events*)
    The phone rings in line 20, and Michelle leaves the house after talking with Nana (line 32).

Incorrect choices:

B Her mother dries her hair (lines 5–6) before the phone rings.

C The coffeemaker starts up (lines 13–14) before the phone rings.

D A neighbor and his puppy walk by (lines 39–40) after Michelle leaves the house.

15. Correct response: **D**
(*Compare and contrast*)
    The sisters talk and giggle when they are outside, but no one in the house talks because they are all busy and it's too noisy.

Incorrect choices:

A Michelle and her sister get ready for school and worry about being on time for the bus, but they don't seem worried about school.

B Mom and Dad seem occupied with their own activities as the girls get ready on their own.

C Both sisters do their homework on the bus (line 46), but they don't seem to be helping each other.

16. Correct response: **B**
(*Use context clues to determine word meaning*)
    To *brandish* means to hold high and wave, as a person might do with a sword. The mother in the poem brandishes a hair dryer as she dries her hair.

Incorrect choices:

A, **C**, and **D** could fit into the sentence (line 5), but they do not fit the meaning of *brandish*.

17. Correct response: **A**
(*Analyze literary elements: theme*)
    As described in the poem, the family's activities are dominated by technology (the radio alarm, the cell alarm, the electric razor, the hair dryer, the toaster, the microwave, e-mail, and even the school bus).

Incorrect choices:

B The children in this poem seem to make decisions on their own, so they don't need more freedom to do so.

C This sentence describes what family members do, but this is not a theme expressed in the poem.

D The children go to school, but the poem does not suggest that this is a child's most important duty.

Carl Linnaeus

18. Correct response: **A**
(*Use suffixes to determine word meaning*)
The suffix -*ist* refers to a person.

Incorrect choices:

B This word is a noun that refers to a person, not an adjective.

C A word that means "against nature" would use the prefix *anti-*.

D A word that means "without nature" would have the suffix -*less*.

19. Correct response: **D**
(*Use details or evidence from the text to support ideas*)
Linnaeus went to Lapland to study plants and became curious about how the people stay so healthy.

Incorrect choices:

A Playing with flowers does not show that someone is curious.

B Difficulty in learning the names of flowers does not indicate curiosity.

C His teachers' opinion was based on his less-than-brilliant performance in school, which would not suggest that he was curious.

20. Correct response: **B**
(*Evaluate author's point of view*)
His system for naming plants was better than the old system and is still in use today.

Incorrect choices:

A This was a new idea at the time but was not a great contribution to science.

C The seventh paragraph says that he went looking for plants to make dyes and medicines, but it does not say he made new discoveries of plants that contributed to science.

D The sixth paragraph says that he noticed something about malaria, but he did not find the cure for it.

21. Correct response: **C**
(*Compare and contrast*)
His plant names were two-part names that made sense, rather than "many Latin words strung together."

Incorrect choices:

A He wrote his book in Swedish, but the plant names were "still in Latin."

B Each name described a group of plants and a characteristic of one plant; Linnaeus named only one flower after himself.

D Some plants were used to make medicines, but they were not named after medicines.

22. Correct response: **C**
(*Identify sequence of events*)
The sixth paragraph says that Linnaeus wrote his final essay about malaria before graduating.

Incorrect choices:

A He wrote this book after graduating from medical school.

B The fifth paragraph says he gave these talks "much later in his life."

D Linnaeus started collecting plants long before he graduated.

23. Correct response: **B**
(*Identify main idea and supporting details*)
The next-to-last paragraph explains the two-part names.

Incorrect choices:

A This is true of the example given in the passage (*Ranunculus acris*) but not for every name.

C The family, or group, is described in the first part of the name.

D This could be described in the second part of the name for one flower, but it would not be the case for every name.

24. Correct response: **A**
(*Draw conclusions*)
He noticed things about plants, about people, and about the causes of malaria, so he must have been a careful observer.

24. (continued)

Incorrect choices:

B He collected plants and knew a lot about them when he was a child, so he was probably not lazy.

C He observed others (such as the Lapps), but there is no evidence that he was suspicious of anyone.

D He graduated from medical school and worked with plants, but there is no evidence that he worked with patients or was an excellent doctor.

The Camera

25. Correct response: **A**
(*Use etymology, root words, and word origins to determine word meaning*)
The root word *spect* means "look or see"; *inspected* means "looked at closely."

Incorrect choices:

B, **C**, and **D** might fit into the sentence, but none is the meaning of the word.

26. Correct response: **D**
(*Analyze characters*)
Manny "shivers" when he sees the image because he is smart enough to realize right away that his camera shows the future.

Incorrect choices:

A His reaction could suggest that he is smart or frightened, but not dreamy.

B There is no evidence to suggest that he is angry.

C Manny "shivers" when he sees the image but not because he is cold.

27. Correct response: **B**
(*Analyze literary elements: plot*)
Manny first realizes that the camera is unusual when he looks at the picture and sees that the kitten is full-grown.

27. (continued)

Incorrect choices:

A He does not know that the camera is unusual when he first sees it.

C He photographs the forsythia after he realizes the camera is unusual.

D He reads the headline after he photographs the forsythia.

28. Correct response: **A**
(*Make inferences*)
Manny knows he is young and his real story will not sound believable, but he wants the assistant to trust him and believe what he says.

Incorrect choices:

B Manny is worried about the accident, not about getting into trouble.

C There is no evidence in the story to support this idea.

D He might enjoy making up stories, but this is not why he gives a false explanation.

29. Correct response: **D**
(*Identify literary devices*)
A "hundred miles an hour" is an exaggeration, but the fact that his heart was pounding faster than usual means that he was afraid.

Incorrect choices:

A He was already standing next to the phone.

B Manny was making a phone call, not pounding or hitting anything.

C A rapid heartbeat could indicate illness, but that is not what this sentence means.

30. Correct response: **A**
(*Interpret figurative language*)
This is a metaphor comparing the blossoming forsythia bush to a fountain.

30. (continued)
Incorrect choices:

B The word *fountain* might suggest water, but that is not what the phrase means.

C This is a literal definition of the phrase but not its real meaning.

D The flowers have already bloomed; they are "blossoms."

31. Correct response: **D**
(*Evaluate author's purpose*)
This is a fantasy story written to entertain.

Incorrect choices:

A This passage was not written to explain accidents.

B This passage is a story, not an article written to inform.

C This passage was written to be entertaining, not persuasive.

32. Correct response: **C**
(*Summarize*)
This is the most complete summary of the story.

Incorrect choices:

A Manny thinks of heroes in comic books, but this is only a detail in the story.

B and **D** are details in the story, not a summary.

Snowstorms Affect New Year's Festivities and Making a Chinese Lantern

33. Correct response: **B**
(*Use reference aids to clarify meaning: dictionary*)
The people were stuck at the railway station in a "helpless position" and could not leave.

Incorrect choices:

A, **C**, and **D** do not fit the context of the sentence.

34. Correct response: **B**
(*Use text features*)
In the fifth paragraph, the lantern festival is described as the "height of the festivities."

Incorrect choices:

A This section does not mention the lantern festival.

C This section tells about travel problems at New Year's, not festivals.

D This section tells of damage caused by the storm.

35. Correct response: **C**
(*Use text features*)
Mr. Liu was one of the people who wanted to travel home for New Year's but did not get there.

Incorrect choices:

A This section does not mention Mr. Liu.

B This section tells about festivities during New Year's.

D This section tells of damage caused by the storm.

36. Correct response: **B**
(*Make connections*)
Making a lantern out of paper is most similar to making a basket with strips of paper. Both activities involve cutting and folding (and probably gluing) paper.

Incorrect choices:

A Making a bowl out of clay does not involve cutting or folding paper.

C A jack-o'-lantern might seem similar to a Chinese lantern, but a Chinese lantern is not carved and does not give off light.

D Decorating something you already have (an egg) is different from making something new.

37. Correct response: **D**
(*Use details or evidence from the text to support ideas*)

The fact that millions of people travel at this time supports the idea that it is the year's most important holiday.

Incorrect choices:

A This detail refers to any time of the year, not just New Year's.

B This detail describes the time of the holiday but not its importance.

C This detail describes one aspect of the holiday but not its importance.

38. Correct response: **A**
(*Distinguish fact and opinion*)

This sentence expresses a personal view that cannot be verified as fact.

Incorrect choices:

B This is a factual statement that can be proven true.

C This is a direction telling what to do and does not express an opinion.

D This sentence describes what you can do if you wish, but it does not express an opinion.

39. Correct response: **B**
(*Identify cause and effect*)

The lantern is cut from a flat piece of paper. When you tape the edges of the paper, it becomes a cylinder (in the shape of a circle).

Incorrect choices:

A The length of the paper does not change when you tape the edges.

C The handle is added in step 6.

D The lantern is hung in step 7.

40. Correct response: **C**
(*Make connections*)

Both of these passages emphasize the importance of the Chinese New Year.

Incorrect choices:

A Lanterns are mentioned in Passage 1, but only Passage 2 emphasizes that you can make them.

B This point is mentioned only in Passage 1.

D Only Passage 1 mentions that more than 1 billion people live in China.

Standardized Test Tutor: Reading

Student Scoring Chart

Grade **5**

Student Name _____

Teacher Name _____

Test 1	Item Numbers	Number Correct/Total	Percent (%)
"The Card Maker" (realistic fiction)	1–5	/5	
"Hatching Eggs Without a Hen" (informational)	6–11	/6	
"Ronald the Painter" (poem)	12–17	/6	
"Police Arrest Unruly Neighbors" (news article)	18–24	/7	
"The Birth of the Green World" (myth)	25–32	/8	
"Bread" and "Oatmeal Bread" (informational)	33–40	/8	
Total	**1–40**	**/40**	

Test 2	Item Numbers	Number Correct/Total	Percent (%)
"Fungi" (informational)	1–5	/5	
"The First Music" (myth)	6–11	/6	
"Seeing the Moon" (poem)	12–17	/6	
"From the *Darnell Elementary School Eagle*" (persuasive essay)	18–24	/7	
"Summer Camp" (realistic fiction)	25–32	/8	
"Jane Goodall" and "Chimpanzees" (informational)	33–40	/8	
Total	**1–40**	**/40**	

Test 3	Item Numbers	Number Correct/Total	Percent (%)
"Kasim's Lesson" (folktale)	1–5	/5	
"Make Your Own Butter" (how-to)	6–11	/6	
"Morning" (poem)	12–17	/6	
"Carl Linnaeus" (biography)	18–24	/7	
"The Camera" (fantasy)	25–32	/8	
"Snowstorms Affect New Year's Festivities" and "Making a Chinese Lantern" (informational)	33–40	/8	
Total	**1–40**	**/40**	

Standardized Test Tutor: Reading

Classroom Scoring Chart

Grade **5**

Teacher Name _____

Student Name	Test 1	Test 2	Test 3